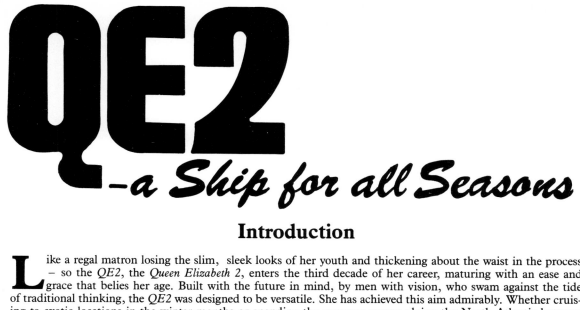

QE2 —a Ship for all Seasons

Introduction

Like a regal matron losing the slim, sleek looks of her youth and thickening about the waist in the process – so the *QE2*, the *Queen Elizabeth 2*, enters the third decade of her career, maturing with an ease and grace that belies her age. Built with the future in mind, by men with vision, who swam against the tide of traditional thinking, the *QE2* was designed to be versatile. She has achieved this aim admirably. Whether cruising to exotic locations in the winter months or spending the summer season plying the North Atlantic between the Old and New Worlds, she is indeed a ship for all seasons.

Perhaps, today, the most famous liner in the world, the *QE2* creates enormous interest in whatever she does and wherever she goes.

It is therefore the purpose of this book to provide an historical background to the ship; to why and how she was built; how she has adapted to change; what she has achieved.

Enjoy the book – enjoy the ship.

David F. Hutchings
Lee-on-the-Solent
Hampshire
June 1988

Dedication

To Sandy I dedicate this book.

Inside Front: The Cunard liner *QE2* on her return to Southampton from her 'shortest ever cruise' to and from the Solent (off Cowes) on 29th April 1987, on the lower swinging ground as she prepares to berth at the Queen Elizabeth II Terminal. The vessel had taken a party of school children on the pleasure trip. The Princess of Wales went on board to join a party given for the young passengers. The Concorde air liner made a low pass as the *QE2* was eased into her berth. *R. Bruce Grice*

Inside Back Cover: Some of the deck plans of the *QE2* as they first appeared in 1969. *Shipbuilding & Shipping Record*

Back Cover: Moonlight and majesty as the *Queen* leaves dry dock in Southampton at 3 a.m. *R.J. Cove*

Front Cover: Queen Elizabeth 2 - Superliner to America. *Cunard*

©David F. Hutchings
Kingfisher Railway Productions
ISBN 0 946184 41 0
June 1988

Typeset by Alphaset
65A The Avenue,
Southampton,
Hants.

Printed by
Amadeus Press
Leeds Road,
Huddersfield,
Yorks.

Contents

Published by
Kingfisher Railway Productions
65A The Avenue, Southampton SO1 2TA

D1127599

Chapter One

A Ship for All Seasons

Cunard's mighty *Queen* liners were growing old. From the years preceding the Second World War the *Queen Mary* – and the *Queen Elizabeth* since – had plied the North Atlantic between Europe and North America with a regularity and luxury that had brought full passenger lists and huge profits to the Cunard Steamship Company.

That is until 1957. In that year the numbers of passengers travelling by sea began to dwindle, the new jet airliners cutting the transatlantic journey from a crossing of four days by ship to just a few hours by air. That particularly fateful year proved to be the fulcrum of the fortunes of many shipping companies as the proportion of passengers being carried by air and sea reached 'evens'. From then on the scale of numbers being carried weighed heavily in favour of the airlines. Over the next decade many ocean liner companies would cease to exist as profits and passengers (especially the tourist and businessman) took to the air, preferring the quicker, time and money-saving passage that came with the aircraft, flying above the bad weather of winter.

Cunard had anticipated that they would eventually have to replace their two beloved *Queen* superliners (these had been the realisation of a long cherished dream to operate a weekly trans-atlantic service with just two express liners). Accordingly, by the late 'fifties, the line had drawn plans for replacements, but the planned ships would be on a 'like-for-like' basis, albeit built with updated technology. Within the company's board of directors there was a hard-core of traditionalists who believed that the aircraft presented no more than a temporary setback to the institution that was Cunard: passengers would always prefer to travel by sea!

The proposed ships would continue the usual North Atlantic trade and be designed purely for the route. No considera-tion was entertained that the ships might go cruising during the unprofitable winter months when the prospect of a rough cross-ing on the notoriously wintery Atlantic, the roughest ocean in the world at that time of year, deterred many a prospective traveller. As passengers sometimes struggled to maintain a footing 'Getting there is half the fun!', Cunard's famous slogan, ceased to have much meaning at that time of year.

By 1959 the designs were advanced far enough for Cunard to approach the Government for financial assistance to enable the company to proceed with their new project. As before with the *Queen Mary* and *Queen Elizabeth* a loan was to be sought which

Leaving Southampton's Ocean Terminal is the magnificent *Queen Elizabeth*. This prima donna of the Atlantic gave her name to the 'New Cunarder'.
Southampton City Museums

Right: Sir John Brocklebank, chairman of Cunard, shakes hands with Sir Matthew Slattery, chairman of BOAC, after signing the BOAC-Cunard agreement on 6th June 1962. Sir Basil Smallpeice (right) was at the time, managing director of BOAC, little realising his future intimate involvement with Cunard.   *British Airways*

Above: A VC10 at London Airport (now Heathrow) proudly shows off its new BOAC-Cunard logo. The lettering of each company's name seems to be in proportion to the number of shares held by each!
British Airways

would similarly be fully repaid, thus making the new ships unique amongst their peers of other nations in being self-sufficient in their operation rather than being subsidised.

The Government, in its turn, formed a committee in September 1959 led by Lord Chandos to consider Cunard's application. After due investigation, two 75,000 ton ships were recommended with speeds of 30 knots and carrying 2,270 passengers.

Soon after the Chandos Committee was formed Cunard's chairman, Colonel Denis Bates, died and Sir John Brocklebank was appointed as his successor.

During the early years of his chairmanship Sir John resurrected an idea that had originally been formulated in the early 'thirties by the then chairman, Sir Percy Bates, to put Cunard into the air business. Subsequently, in 1959, Cunard bought Eagle Airways. In 1960 Cunard – Eagle, as the line would be known, applied for a licence to fly the Atlantic to New York and at the same time purchased two Boeing aircraft to show their determination. The licence was granted, then revoked after an appeal by BOAC.

Although Cunard carried on its air operations from the United Kingdom to Bermuda (and from there to New York etc)

A drawing of 31st March 1961 shows a proposal for the Q3 project. The funnel configuration has not yet been decided but one could assume that it might have been similar to the John Brown-built Swedish liner *Kungsholm* that was launched in 1965.
Based on a drawing supplied by Liverpool University

the company finally came to an arrangement with BOAC in June 1962 and BOAC–Cunard was formed, with the shipping company holding a 30 per cent interest.

Perhaps the Government seeing Cunard spend £8.5 million on this new enterprise had second thoughts as the Chandos Committee now recommended that the company should be granted a loan for the building of only one new ship, designated 'Q3', and that she should be designed solely as a three class North Atlantic express liner. A loan of £17 million, at a low rate of interest, would be made available against the £28 million (maximum) that the new ship would be expected to cost. Many of the younger directors were still unhappy about the type of ship that was being selected and they found an ally in Sir John Brocklebank.

Sir John reappraised the whole situation – dwindling passenger numbers, increasing losses, potential actual cost of the Q3 by the time of building – and took a momentous decision and cancelled the new liner. He later described the decision to build her as a 'disaster'.

A fresh look was taken at the company's requirements and at the advances that had been made in the arts and technologies of shipbuilding, in propulsion machinery and in materials available to the shipbuilder. The new ship, Sir John Brocklebank stated, would not be an updated version of the two existing *Queens* nor would it be a re-working of the Q3 idea.

Sir John liked to refer to the new project as 'The New Cunarder' but the ship soon became known as the 'Q4'. Spike Milligan, that most zany of British comics, parodied the nomenclature theme for a television comedy series – 'Q6'. Other 'Qs' in this popular series followed thereafter.

The initial concept for 'The New Cunarder' was for the 27 and 12 boilers of the *Queen Mary* and *Queen Elizabeth* respectively, and their four propellers each, to be replaced in the Q4 by four boilers and two propellers. Modern engines etc had enabled an almost equal amount of power to be obtained from a smaller installation. Enough fuel would also be carried to last a complete round North Atlantic voyage at an average speed of 28.5 knots. 2,000 passengers, in three classes, would be carried in maximum safety with a corresponding reliability of service. Rooms, too, would be flexible in as much as they could be changed from one class to another, ideal for when cruising.

58,000 gross tons would be contained within the 960 foot hull and a beam of 104 feet would enable the liner to pass through the Panama and Suez Canals with just 18 inches clearance on either side of the former. This, with the ability to produce her own fresh water (the old *Queens* could carry enough only for a few days), would open up the world to the new ship.

The dual role of North Atlantic liner sailing and tropical ocean cruising became increasingly attractive to Cunard.

Q4 – the new 58,000 ton CUNARDER

Advance publicity for No. 736 shows how the liner would be divided, although classes have not been designated.   *Cunard*

4

Chapter Two

Do or Die

Under the relatively short chairmanship of Sir John Brocklebank with his policy of 'new thinking', Cunard diversified its passenger operations.

Although Cunard was still carrying more passengers than any other shipping company, their transatlantic passenger service was developing into an ever increasing loss-maker and it was decided to send some of the other passenger ships in the fleet cruising. The only full-time cruise ship that Cunard operated was the luxurious *Caronia*, popularly known as 'The Dollar Princess' or 'The Green Goddess' because of the three shades of light green in which her hull was painted.

Cunard had also made a study of other Atlantic liners that had been sent cruising during the winter months as an alternative to running with that season's associated reductions in patronage on the northern ocean. The magnificent *France* of the French Line was studied in depth as was the US Lines' *United States*.

Ultimately two of the Cunard's Canadian service ships, *Saxonia* and *Ivernia*, were sent to John Brown's shipbuilding yard in Scotland for extensive rebuilding to convert them into cruise-ships. This was done in 1962, the liners reappearing as the *Carmania* and *Franconia*. The lessons learnt from this pair were of great practical benefit when the facilities and materials to be incorporated in the Q4 were being considered.

The experience in building a third sister, the *Sylvania*, of 1955 had also been of use. Plastic piping, plastic baths, lightweight furniture and specially developed, deeper than usual, girders (which had holes cut into them to enable easy passage of piping and electrical cables) had been used to facilitate the saving of weight and these ideas were to be used to advantage ten years later.

The *Mauretania* too went cruising and, then, in 1963 the mighty *Queens* found winter employment in this lucrative and expanding market. Their great prestige ensured that they were popular in their new roles, although their draughts of 38 feet and beams of 118 feet precluded their access to the harbours of many ports that they visited. Consequently they had to anchor offshore from these prohibited havens, ferrying passengers ashore by their own ship's boats.

It was planned that the Q4 should have a greatly reduced beam and draught in comparison to her predecessors: this was to be made possible by stringent weight saving through the careful use of lighter materials in her construction that had been made available from the very latest advances in technology. Thus the ports made inaccessible to her predecessors would be opened to the new ship, enabling her to moor alongside jetties in sheltered waters and allowing her passengers to disembark directly from ship to shore in comfort.

Cruising from New York, the *Elizabeth* sailed to the Bahamas and sometimes crossed the Atlantic to visit various ports in the Mediterranean. On this side of 'The Pond' the *Mary* sailed from Southampton, rolling her way through the Bay of Biscay with her stabilisers retracted (to conserve fuel en-route) to the Canaries, Lisbon and Gibraltar.

During one flying visit to the *Mary*, whilst she was calling at Cannes during 1966, Sir Basil Smallpeice paid a visit to his counterpart of the French Line who was on board the *France*, anchored a short way from the British ship. From this visit stemmed the idea of operating the 'Lizzie', and later the Q4, in mutual co-operation with the *France* instead of in competition. It was also planned that the *Mary* and *Elizabeth* should be kept in service until 1968 and 1969 respectively before withdrawing them. The 'Lizzie' would be kept on the route for a year longer than the *Mary* in order to provide the Q4 with a running mate. Commodore Geoffrey Marr was to keep the *Elizabeth* as his flagship with the captaincy of the Q4 passing to William ('Bil with one 'l' ') Warwick who would also stand by 'The New Cunarder' whilst she was being built.

But in 1966, because of its passenger fleet losses of the previous few years (only slightly alleviated in the early years of the decade by the more healthy revenue derived from the profits of its cargo operations before they, too, declined), Cunard's financial position deteriorated even further. This, combined with a £4 million loss caused by the lengthy seaman's strike of that year, forced the company to once more reappraise its position. An innovation for the company occurred with a switch to containerisation when Cunard joined, in December 1966, the Atlantic Container Line which saved the cargo business by its resultant profitability.

Sir Basil Smallpeice had by this time taken over the helm of the company and he proceeded to take the policy of Sir John Brocklebank's 'New thinking' to its brilliantly successful — albeit extremely unpopular at the time — conclusion. By re-thinking the new policies he arrived at the conclusion that ships should not merely be used as a means of getting from 'A' to 'B' but should be used as part of the journey, a hotel that took its passengers to places whilst, meanwhile, enjoying themselves during the passage.

Perhaps spurred on by shrewd observations from senior staff such as the fleet's newly appointed Commodore, Geoffrey Marr, who pointed out that the shore staff and offices had not

Carinthia and *Caronia* (The 'Green Goddess'), the last Cunard ships to go before 'Q4' came into service. *Norman Jackman*

The *Queen Mary*, the epitome of the ocean liner, leaves Southampton for the last time on 31st October 1967 en-route to preservation and a whole new career in Long Beach, California.   *Southampton City Museums*

been trimmed to match the needs of the fleet and that in many instances posts and functions were excessively overmanned, Sir Basil put further economies into practice, convinced that to be a viable proposition the company had 'to do or die'.

Older ships and those not converted for cruising were sold (after the sale of the *Caronia* in May 1968 only the *Carmania* and *Franconia* were left); the main passenger office was moved from Liverpool to Southampton (March 1967); offices in many towns were shut and sold and Cunard's interest in BOAC – Cunard were bought back by BOAC, realising a handsome profit for the shipping company.

But the heaviest decision of all came as a blow to Britain generally: the beloved *Queens* were to be retired one year earlier than had been anticipated.

The *Mary* was withdrawn first on 20th September 1967. On board the old liner Captain John Treasure Jones, himself facing his own retirement, toasted a portrait of the 'New Cunarder' that was being launched in Scotland that day; on the 22nd the liner left New York for the last time after due honours had been paid to her by the city's Mayor, leaving behind a sadness and a void in the city that has never since been filled.

Everyone was losing 'their' *Queen*. As the three-funnelled Atlantic liner headed towards home, and a continuation of her destiny, she passed the *Queen Elizabeth* for the last time just after midnight in mid-Atlantic on September 25th. The sister ships bade a poignant, final farewell to each other with their mighty whistles as their illuminated funnels flashed on and off.

The *Mary* had been sold for £1.25 million to the City of Long Beach and, after a final short cruise from Southampton, sailed for her new home on October 31st, via Cape Horn, where she was refurbished as the 'Hotel Queen Mary', being rebuilt in some areas as an attraction centre. Well looked-after, she is still there – a legacy of art deco and luxury from the days when the sea track was the only highway between Europe and the USA.

A different fate awaited the *Queen Elizabeth*, however. It had been intended to sail her in conjunction with the Q4 for at least a year after the latter ship's introduction into service but a combination of Cunard's financial circumstances exacerbated by the seamens' strike and the partnership between the *Queen* and the *France*, which could be carried over to the new ship, caused her premature demise.

Sold to a somewhat 'shady' American consortium she left Southampton in circumstances very different from the emotive but affectionate farewell given to the *Mary*: it seemed as if she was being banished, sailing almost furtively, in the early morning fog. It had been planned to keep her in Philadelphia but she languished for two years, gradually rotting, at Port Everglades near Fort Lauderdale in Florida. After this interlude of despair she was again offered for sale and found a buyer in C.Y. Tung of Hong Kong.

Sailing from Florida in August of 1970 she was renamed *Seawise University*, undergoing conversion to a cruising university in Hong Kong.

Before she even once sailed in her new role she caught fire in several places at once and, after blazing for several days, rolled over and died. As in the mid-60s Cunard had spent $4m converting her for cuising and installing fire prevention standards to US regulations it was considered that the cause of destruction had been sabotage. A sad ending to the world's finest and largest ship, a symbol of Britain's post war recovery in the days of austerity and rationing.

Throughout this financially and emotionally complex period with its cut-backs at sea and the closure, sale or transfer of shore offices the main aims of the stringent rationalisation were carefully nurtured until they reached fruition with the survival of Cunard and the tangible result of the 'new thinking' – the planning and building of the most versatile liner that the world had yet seen.

On 19th August 1964 the Cunard line invited five shipbuilders to tender for the construction of the 'New Cunarder' and by 30th November the bids had been returned. Within one month the final choice had been made and the contract to build Q4 was awarded to the John Brown shipyard of Clydebank (the former builders of the *Queen Mary* and *Queen Elizabeth*) as their tender of £25,427,000 was the best received.

Just after 3pm, on 30th December within the augustly solid surroundings of the Bank of England, Sir John Brocklebank (then still chairman of the steamship company) and Lord Aberconway, chairman of John Brown and Company (Clydebank) Limited, signed the contract.

The initial contract called for a twin screw ship of 28.5 knots (less speed would be required for cruising), with four boilers and catering for the American, as well as the traditional, demand for three classes. One boiler was dispensed with during a later cost-cutting exercise and, in order to cut down on kitchen logistics and to provide an easier operating environment for cruising (when the ship would become one class), the ship sensibly also became a two-class vessel. These changes were decided upon even whilst the ship was building, an early indication of the design's versatility.

Cunard, it seemed, was set fair on a course for recovery and all bade well for the future – once the ship was completed.

But there were still shoals ahead.

Within the solid walls of the Bank of England on 30th December 1964, Sir John Brocklebank (for Cunard) and Lord Aberconway (for John Brown, Clydebank) sign the building contract for Q4 - the 'New Cunarder'. *Cunard*

Chapter Three

Building for the Future

July 2nd 1965 dawned a beautiful, bright day over the expectant shipyard of John Brown and Company Limited. The keel of No. 736, the shipyard's order-book number for the 'New Cunarder', was due to be laid on the short length of wooden blocks that would eventually be extended down to the water's edge along the length of No. 4 slipway, the birthplace of many a Cunard ship, including the two mighty *Queens*. She was to be Cunard's 172nd ship and her keel laying was to take place just two days before the 125th anniversary of the company's founding by Samuel Cunard of Halifax, Nova Scotia.

From this neat row of blocks extended six baulks of timber placed horizontally at right angles to, and erected level with, the top of the blocks. To one side of the building blocks a prefabricated section of the new ship's keel and double bottom rested on these baulks and other temporary blocks waiting to be ceremoniously slid into place.

John Rannie, the managing director of the shipyard whose crowning achievement the Q4 would be (he would be retiring when the ship was finally handed over to Cunard), had stipulated that the prefabricated section being built in the workshops should weigh forty tons. This would be within the combined lifting capabilities of two tower cranes adjoining the slip which, with the aid of a powerful winch fixed to the concrete base of a long vanished derrick crane, would lift and pull the keel section into place.

At least, that was the plan.

Lady Aberconway, the wife of John Brown's chairman, had agreed to perform the ceremony and various reporters had been invited along to witness the occasion. At the appointed time the cranes took the strain of the steel section and the winch commenced to take in the slack on the wire cables. Unfortunately the cranes were designed to lift their maximum load of 20 tons each in a vertical direction and not at the angle induced by the pull on the winch.

After moving slightly the keel section refused to move any further which placed an enormous strain on the winch. Consequently, as the winch continued to pull in its cable, the entire concrete block into which it was fixed started a process of being extracted from the earth, dried out during recent fine weather.

The ceremony thus came to a hasty and slightly undignified halt and the pressmen were quickly ushered into the Model Room where they were liberally entertained.

The recalcitrant keel section was quietly eased into position onto the building blocks on the following Monday, 5th July, by a carefully chosen gang of men who had delayed their start of the local 'Clydebank Fair'; the shipyard was normally closed-down during the fortnight of this annual holiday.

After an initial public embarrasment, the keel of No. 736 was quietly slid into place on Monday 5th July 1967.   *Boyd Haining*

Even before the contract had been signed an air of confidence that the company would be given the contract to build Q4 had existed within the boardroom of John Brown's. This confidence, almost mounting to an assumption, was based on the Company's record of building many previous famous Cunarders such as the *Lusitania*, *Aquitania* and, of course, the *Queen Mary* and *Queen Elizabeth*. The prevailing confidence even extended to the pronouncement of an early delivery date for the completed 'New Cunarder': one which would have unhappy consequences.

During the months preceding the laying of the first few symbolic tons of the new 736, a mass of work had already taken place. Calculations, drawings, estimates and planning, the preparation of network charts (showing in a numerical and time form what job had to be done, in which order and when – in

Many funnel designs were considered and tested at John Brown's. Here some of the designs are shown together.
University of Liverpool, Cunard Archives

The liner's novel funnel design, shown here on a large model, with added arrows graphically showing the wind direction induced by the windscoop and casing.
University of Liverpool, Cunard Archives

order to avoid 'bottlenecks' and hold-ups) had all been started. The advance ordering of much material had also gone ahead and the basic design principles had been established. These latter criteria would not be changed, whatever else was, and included positions of support pillars, bulkheads and, most importantly, the location of engines. This was determined as being just aft of amidships (for stability and strength): in turn this dictated funnel location which, being placed almost amidships, allowed the development of a dual purpose series of terraced decks, cascading down through five decks towards the stern, providing shelter during North Atlantic passages and offering delightful sun-traps whilst cruising.

Heading Cunard's design team were their naval architect, Dan Wallace, and technical director, marine engineer Tom Kameen. Dan Wallace had served his apprenticeship in the esteemed shipyard to which he now returned, finding himself senior to those who had once been his peers.

John Brown's own prestigious but secretive design office was led by the yard's technical director, John Stark, who also had responsibility for the yard's experimental tank in which were tested differing hull models of the new liner until one had been perfected. On the forefoot of the ship a 'bulb' would be fitted; this bulbous bow would 'punch a hole' in the water ahead of the ship thereby cutting down water resistance on the hull – and also cut down the fuel bills. The traditional bow wave, beloved of all marine artists, would disappear, robbing Q4 of her 'bone in the teeth' when she was underway.

Cunard's naval architect, Dan Wallace (right), discusses a point of the Q4's design.
University of Liverpool, Cunard Archives

From the initial laying of the keel the erection of steelwork on No. 4 slip went on at a steady pace. Extra men were taken on when necessary and if they did not hold any documentary evidence that they were competent at their trade then they were given a test task.

To maintain an adequate supply of steel sections (such as angle-bar and tee-bar) the steel mills in the vicinity of Clydebank would give advance notice of their rolling dates of particular sections to the drawing office so that sufficient time could be allowed for ordering. Weekly co-ordinating visits by John Brown's commercial manager to the mills also ensured that a flow of information was maintained.

Aluminium alloy was to be used in great quantities in the construction of the superstructure once the steel hull had been completed. 1,100 tons, the largest amount (including some of the biggest plates) ever used on a British liner, were to be supplied by Alcan who organised a special training centre within the yard. The trained welders were also periodically checked for standards of workmanship which thus remained high throughout the building of the ship.

Above: Several differing models of the Q4's hull were built and tested in John Brown's towing tank. One model is shown being put through its paces in simulated rough weather conditions.
University of Liverpool, Cunard Archives.

Left: 1,100 tons of aluminium was to be used in the liner's superstructure and much of it was prefabricated in the shipyard's workshops.
University of Liverpool, Cunard Archives

A workshop for the preparation of the aluminium plates (of which many were delivered in ready-to-use sizes) was specially dedicated for this purpose having its floor treated with a special sealant to prevent any foreign particles affecting the metal. As soon as the aluminium was prepared and welded into prefabricated units it was primed with a special anti-corrosion paint and this remained superbly effective throughout construction.

The use of aluminium (along with other innovative weight saving design features) had enabled the design team to reduce the liner's draught by several feet than if steel had been used in the superstructure. It also enabled the number of decks to be increased from 12 in the old *Queens* to 13 in the Q4.

The addition of an extra passenger deck more than compensated for the limits on length and beam that had been imposed by the planned usage of the Panama and Suez Canals. This additional deck had also been made possible by the reduction of 6 to 9 inches in the heights of other decks by running electrical cables, piping and ventilation trunking over main passageways and bathrooms where a lower headroom was acceptable. Cunard's engineering staff had also managed to save a creditable 3 feet in the height of the machinery spaces.

Lloyd's ship surveyors were also keenly interested in the superstructure as it was to be regarded as part of the ship's strength structure. Accordingly, expansion joints (the narrow, protected transverse 'gaps' in the uppermost deck of a ship that allowed the superstructure to 'work' in heavy weather when the main hull bends) were omitted.

To prevent any corrosive electrolytic interaction between the steel of the hull and the aluminium superstructure a careful bonding method had to be utilised. A special epoxy compound was spread along the joints between the two metals and then steel rivets were used for the final connection.

Left: Surrounded by a web of scaffolding, the curved stem and bulbous bow already display their elegant curves. *Boyd Haining*

Below: Partially built from prefabricated sections, these deck houses on the boat deck will soon accommodate the Double Up Room, shops and theatre balcony. *University of Liverpool, Cunard Archives*

The various weight saving exercises proved to be a worthwhile – and potentially profitable – operation but it also affected the centre of gravity which, as a consequence, had to be lowered. The usual method of remedying this problem would have been to add, in the Q4's case, 750 tons of otherwise useless ballast to the bottom of the ship. But the designers ingeniously did away with the use of this dead weight and instead turned it to advantage.

Their solution was to increase certain steel plate thicknesses in areas where greater than usual wear (or corrosion) could be reasonably expected to occur, such as in the lower most structure in way of machinery and the fore part of hull, strengthening it against ice. Increasing the weight of steel work within the double bottom by constructing more closely subdivided double bottom cells also added to the ship's strength.

Of the many thousands of items that were to be fitted into the hull of No. 736, many had to be made specially for the liner.

The propulsion machinery – boilers, turbines, gearboxes, condensers and propeller shafts – and much ancilliary machinery was made by John Brown Engineering (Clydebank) Limited but built under licences from the respective designers or developers. Much of the machinery had been conceived in its original form in the years succeeding 1954 when the idea of replacements for the *Mary* and *Elizabeth* were first mooted, culminating in the ill-fated Q3 project. The Q3 designs were resurrected and modified until the machinery for the Q4 was finally chosen. Reliability, simplicity and efficiency were to be the watchwords.

Twenty seven boilers in the *Queen Mary* and twelve in the *Queen Elizabeth* had given 160,000 shaft horse power to four propellers (40,000 shp each) to give a service speed of 28.5 knots.

Left: With launching cradle in place and with new paint gleaming, the bow of the 'Q4' towers above the slipway.
University of Liverpool, Cunard Archives

Below: One of the two 19-foot six-bladed propellers, each weighing 31 tons 13 cwt (32,157 hg), poised above the tidal Clyde. Each of these propellers would absorb 55,000 shp to give a service speed the same as the old Cunard *Queens*. *University of Liverpool, Cunard Archives*

Advances in marine engineering had been such that the Q4 was to have four watertube boilers which would deliver 120,000 shp giving the same speed from only two propellers. The propeller manufacturers, Stone Manganese Marine of Greenwich, were concerned at the amount of power that each of their products would have to absorb and were greatly relieved when, because of economies, the four boilers were reduced to three. 110,000 shp would now be produced, giving the same service speed.

The boilers were of Foster Wheeler ESD II design and, at 278 tons each, were the largest ever constructed for a marine installation. Steam was produced at 850 pounds per square inch at a temperature of 950°F (later rising to 1,000°F).

The steam was fed into two sets of turbines (double reduction, double helical, dual tandem gearing) which were built to a design by Pametrada Limited. Pametrada or, to give its proper title, Parsons Marine Engineering Turbine Research and Development Association (supported by shipbuilding and various marine turbine engineering firms) was the successor to the firm founded by the inventor of the turbine, Sir Charles Parsons.

The magazine 'Engineering' described the turbines: 'Each set is a two-cylinder unit, in which the flow from the high-pressure turbine feeds one double-flow low-pressure turbine, exhausting into an underslung condenser. The turbines are connected to the main shaft by a dual tandem arrangement of double helical gears'.

Amongst many companies that produced other machinery for various purposes AEI built three turbine-generators which would produce the ship's life forces, steam and electricity, for the various ship's services. Many years later AEI, as part of the GEC group, would have a further major involvement in the life of the liner.

However, to ensure that the maximum, most efficient use was obtained from the available machinery space, a scale model was made showing the positions of every pipe and piece of gear.

The 'New Cunarder', like her predecessors before her, loomed over her surroundings during her building. Because she was practically all-welded the traditional sounds of rivetting no longer sent their staccato rhythms out over Clydebank.

There was a quietness in the town, a silent overture to the coming years of change.

One of the many items contracted-out to smaller firms. Here one of the propeller cones is about to leave Southampton-based Hardingham Pressure Vessels Ltd. for Glasgow. *Roger Hardingham*

Two sets of stabilisers were built into No. 736 enabling, amongst other things, the restaurants to be carried higher in the ship.
Boyd Haining

Diagram showing the high pressure ahead turbine and astern turbine. Because of the high temperatures involved, stainless iron blades were used.
Engineering Magazine

Chapter Four

Fourteen to One

Yard No. 736 rested sleek and serene on the stocks of Slip Number 4.

Her Majesty, Queen Elizabeth II, had graciously consented to launch the new liner and for many weeks previous to the chosen day a great deal of conjecture surrounded the possible name of the new ship.

Many suggestions had been put forward: *Princess Anne, Queen of Britain, British Queen, Queen Victoria* (a name previously mooted for the subsequently named *Queen Mary*), *Britannia* (Cunard's first ship), *Prince Charles, New Britain, John F. Kennedy* and *Churchill* were amongst the more serious contenders that found varying odds in the betting shops.

Perhaps it was because one *Queen Elizabeth* was still in service that that particular name did not attract much attention for the new ship. Odds of 14 to 1 were offered. Her Majesty's own name (although Queen Elizabeth II of England she was yet Queen Elizabeth I of Scotland) did not figure high in the betting stakes.

Even at this eleventh hour before the launch there had been anxious moments in the higher echelons of Cunard. A loss of £3.5 million had just been announced on the passenger ship operations and, to aggravate matters even more, an increase in the cost of Q4 was expected to be in the region of £4 million. (A final price of £29,091,000 would eventually be agreed in later months).

The £17.6 million loan that the company had secured from the Government was clearly not going to be enough, so Sir Basil Smallpeice met Sir Harold Lever, Financial Secretary to the Treasury, on September 13th, just one week before the launch date.

The result announced on the 14th was an increase of the original loan to £24 million and the day was saved. The £24 million was later reduced by £4 million when Cunard found that the full amount was not eventually needed. This was because the sales of the *Carinthia, Sylvania, Queen Elizabeth* and *Caronia* in 1968 realised £7 million. This would leave, other than Q4, only two ships in service, the *Carmania* and *Franconia*, and the three ships would be marketed by the newly-formed Cunard Line Limited.

So, not only did Cunard still have a business that they were once in danger of losing but they had a new ship and a new hope for the future, all won by so much drastic economic surgery of ships and men.

Q4 almost ready for launching as seen from the Clyde.

Steam and Sail

Her Majesty The Queen, HRH Prince Philip, The Duke of Edinburgh, and Lord Aberconway, Chairman of John Brown Shipyard, pause during a tour of the slip prior to the launching of No. 736. Sir Basil Smallpeice, Chairman of Cunard, stands to the left.

University of Liverpool, Cunard Archives

The mood of a revived Cunard seemed to be reflected by the sunshine that greeted the Queen on her arrival at Clydebank on 20th September 1967.

The launch of the 'New Cunarder', like the launches of her illustrious predecessors, had occupied the talk of the people of the upper reaches of the Clyde for many a day, and thousands flocked to the yard or to the fields on the opposite side of the Clyde, to view the proceedings.

The weather was made ideal by a light westerly wind which helped to ensure that the required depth of water would be available at the end of the standing ways in good time for the launch. Wind of another 5 knots would have presented a problem, however.

Stewards were posted at various points within the viewing compounds and at various danger points such as at cranes where individuals could be deterred from climbing them to obtain a better view.

Princess Margaret (she had previously opened an exhibition of the Q4's specially designed fitments at the Design Centre) had arrived in Glasgow on the eve of the launch, touring the launch slipway the following day. Her early appearance increased the odds on the selection of her name for the liner.

John Brown's managing director, John Rannie, greeted the Queen on her arrival, outshining Sir Basil Smallpeice and his own chairman, Lord Aberconway, as her host. After introducing Her Majesty to various leading figures involved with Q4, John Rannie accompanied the Queen on her tour to inspect the launching trigger which she would soon be remotely activating.

The launching party then ascended to the platform at the very bow of the ship, against which the bottle of champagne would shortly be splitting and frothing.

Continuing the traditions of the launching ceremony the Queen was handed an envelope containing a sheet of paper on which was written the long-kept secret – the proposed name of the new liner. (The written reminder of the ship's name had become a considered necessity ever since an august personage had forgotten the name of the ship to be launched!) A similar envelope had been deposited in the safe at Cunard's New York office, just in case of a breakdown in communications. Her Majesty refused the proferred envelope. 'I won't be needing that!' she joked, then spoke clearly into the microphones: 'I name this ship *Queen Elizabeth the Second*. May God bless her and all who sail in her'. It was 2:28pm.

A great roar went up from several thousand throats as the Queen cut the ribbon, using the same gold scissors that her mother and grandmother had previously used in the performance of launching their Royal namesakes, releasing the christening wine that stiffly swung its way to destruction. A button was then pressed that electrically released the launching trigger that kept a last land-locked hold on the mighty hull.

The Queen, the first reigning British monarch to launch a liner, had used her intuition to name the ship. The envelope that she had refused – and the one in New York – had contained the name *Queen Elizabeth*.

After the launch Sir Basil Smallpeice consulted with the Queen's Private Secretary Sir (later Lord) Michael Adeane and it was decided that the suffix 'Second' would be written as the Arabic '2', and not as the Roman 'II'.

This was done for several reasons. Firstly, it was good publicity; secondly, only battleships had carried a reigning monarch's Romanic suffix, thirdly, the ship was to be the second ship to bear the name *Queen Elizabeth*, a nice deference to both the Queen and the Queen Mother after whom the first *Lizzie* had been named as Queen Consort; and, fourthly – and perhaps most importantly – the Queen was still, in fact, only Queen Elizabeth I of Scotland and to name the ship with 'II' would have been an insult to the people of the country that had now produced a fitting successor to the Queens *Mary* and *Elizabeth*.

As the last wedges retaining the ship on the slip were knocked away, the ship seemed to stick on the well-greased standing ways and only to the trained eye did she apparently move. A voice shouted, 'Give her a push!' and George Parker, the shipyard director, stepped forward and jokingly did so! Slowly at first, then with an ever increasing momentum, the *QE2* slid over tons of tallow towards her fast-approaching element.

Bundles of drag chains, weighing hundreds of tons in total (which had lain neatly alongside the launching ways, attached to the hull cables and later-to-be-removed eye bolts) gradually moved into rattling, clanking motion as the ship pulled them with her towards the specially-dredged River Clyde. The purpose of these bundles was to slow the ship down as she entered the water on this the first, short – but most dangerous – journey of her life, and to prevent her ramming the opposite bank of the river with her stern.

As the new *Queen* touched the water a perfectly timed anchor-formation of aircraft from the appropriately designated No. 736 Squadron of the Fleet Air Arm flew overhead.

The many hundreds of people in the fields opposite the shipyard had been warned by the police that the expected mini-tidal wave generated by the liner's entry into the water would

Above: Just minutes before the launch. The Q4 stands proud and ready on No. 4 slipway.
University of Liverpool, Cunard Archives

Left: At 2.30 pm on 20th September 1967 No. 736 is launched by Her Majesty Queen Elizabeth II. The liner would now be known as *Queen Elizabeth 2*, the QE2. A crowd of thousands watch as the liner takes to the water for the first time.
University of Liverpool, Cunard Archives.

Nearing completion, the liner is freshly painted and almost ready for launching. *Boyd Haining*

A trip to the fields on the opposite side of the Clyde to the shipyard always proved a worthwhile journey. Shipbuilding and agriculture are indelibly intertwined in this evocative photograph. *Boyd Haining*

From the opposite bank of the Clyde the *QE2* is seen to advantage as she makes contact with the water.
University of Liverpool, Cunard Archives.

probably flood the edge of the fields in which they stood. But once the launch was over the crowd moved forward to watch the 'New Cunarder', the *QE2*, as she was taken into care by tugs. Ushered towards the fitting-out jetty which would be her home for several months to follow, she would here take on the apparel appropriate for the world's newest *Queen*.

Meanwhile the official launch party headed towards the specially refurbished Mould Loft where a champagne afternoon tea had been arranged. A luncheon had been precluded because of the time of the launch and by the Royal party's programme.

Boyd Haining, then shipyard manager, remembers the tea as 'a delightful affair consisting of dainty sandwiches in variety, and gooey cakes and gateaux. Toasts were taken in champagne selected by Aberconway, knowing HM's taste. The champagne was a heady one – Krug Privee Curee, demi-sec, vintage 1961'.

In his chairman's post-launch speech Lord Aberconway voiced what would in effect be the beginning of the end of John Brown's shipyard as an independent entity. He said that the *QE2* would be the last ship of note of which it could be said 'she was a John Brown ship'. Economics were again at work.

He continued:
'We have announced, with our friends and neighbours on the upper Clyde, that we intend to merge our shipbuilding interests. Without question this would be to the advantage of shipbuilding on the Clyde, of continued employment on the river, and of the country's economy. But it does carry with it the consequence that there will pass from the scene of shipbuilding the name of John Brown, a name which (though I should not say it) is second to none in fame and repute. This yard will go on, playing a major part in a wider shipbuilding setting, and will contribute its skills and traditions to the new organisation of which it will be part. Many great ships will be built and fitted out at Clydebank in the years to come, to the same standards as in the last seventy 'John Brown' years; they will be worthy successors to the *Queen Mary*, the *Queen Elizabeth* and the *Queen Elizabeth the Second*.'

The Queen, in her speech, said:
'I particularly welcome the opportunity you have given me to launch this splendid successor to those two famous Cunarders *Queen Mary* and *Queen Elizabeth*. I suppose these two ships were better known and loved, both in peace and war, by all of us living in these islands, than any other merchantman in our history. I have always had a special affection for them because they were named after my grandmother and my mother, and it does not seem so very long ago that I was present with my sister when my mother launched the *Queen Elizabeth*.

Every great enterprise has an element of risk and uncertainty about it, and I am sure no-one can predict the future career of the new Cunarder. I am equally certain that, in the experienced and capable hands of the Cunard company, she will stand the best chance of a happy and profitable lifetime.'

The element of risk and uncertainty of which the Queen spoke would be realised sooner than any of those present could predict.

Of the proposed, and hopefully beneficial, amalgamation of the upper Clyde shipyards the Queen remarked:
'We have all read, with a touch of nostalgia, that the name of John Brown is to disappear from the list of great shipbuilders. However, this does not mean that the very special skill and spirit of this yard will be lost to Clydeside or to British shipbuilding. In wishing the *Queen Elizabeth the Second* a long life and good fortune on all her voyages, I add my best wishes for success and prosperity to the new consortium of Clydeside shipbuilders.'

Instead of the usual piece of jewellery the Queen was then presented with a new motor launch for the Royal Yacht *Britannia*. 'I suppose we ought to paint it in Cunard colours and call it *John Brown*!' said Her Majesty. 'Why not paint it brown and call it *Cunard*!' retorted a wit at the top table.'

Within a very short time, under the recommendations of the Geddes Committee, John Brown would become the Clydebank division of Upper Clyde Shipbuilders. It would be under the regime of this new consortium under the chairmanship of Tony Hepper but with John Rannie still in direct control of the *QE2* project, that the liner would be finished.

Chapter Five

The Element of Risk

The liner lay berthed alongside the fitting out jetty, her empty compartments soon to be transformed into carpeted rooms of luxury or hygienically tiled storerooms and kitchens.

But meanwhile she contained a bustle of men and machines. Cables lay like black snakes along the decks or hanging down from overhead and the shouts and calls of the skilled workforce filled the corridors, rooms and machinery spaces as they went about their myriad tasks.

Fitting, inspecting and testing carried on, day in, day out until, part by part, the *QE2* metamorphosed from what appeared to be chaos to the casual viewer, to a unity of practical beauty.

The *QE2* was to be a showpiece for Great Britain, for her country's art, design and engineering skills, not only now in the late 1960s but in the decades to follow. Her decor had not only to be modern but futuristic; it had to anticipate tastes for years to come – an almost impossible task for the designers involved.

But it was done.

In the past the interior decoration had almost been left to chance and a hotchpotch of styles were used that, as a whole, sometimes lacked unity.

Sometimes a chairman's wife might be given the task of choosing materials; in large ships renowned architects, more used to designing country mansions, were also appointed and the resultant decor in the ships' lounges and restaurants would reflect the lavish days of Imperial Rome, Classical Greece or elegant, timbered English mansions. The sea outside was almost deliberately forgotten.

The *Queen Mary* had perfectly reflected the art of the 1930s in her Art-Deco, architectural interiors (her 'Ocean Liner' style becoming more popularly known as 'Odeon') but these had soon dated. The *Queen Elizabeth* became the symbol of British post-war recovery and great things were done with the available materials. But she too, partially reflected pre-war design and was stylishly and architecturally luxurious.

Safely berthed alongside the fitting-out jetty, the *QE2* takes on the appareil of a luxury liner, still surrounded by the bustle of the shipyard.

Scottish Record Office

Mr. James Gardner had overall responsibility for the 'New Cunarder's' interior design and exterior appearance.

Shipbuilding & Shipping Record

QE2 would be everything inside and out. She would reflect the art and technology of the 1960s whilst being timeless. She would also have a carefully built-in versatility rather than built-in architecture that would enable her to change to reflect new tastes and styles.

The style of the 'Swinging 1960s' that had made Britain the leader in world design and fashion, along with the bright, colour awareness which had been distilled and matured from the early 1960s, all helped to create the feel of the *QE2*. To ensure that the best in design was made available to Cunard the Council of Industrial Design was consulted.

Lady Brocklebank, wife of Cunard's chairman at the time when Q4's contract was signed, had originally been appointed to lead a team of designers. Her wide experience of travel, of ships and hotels ('I know what people like and dislike' she once said) made her admirably qualified for the post.

Lady Brocklebank disappeared from the scene upon the retirement through ill-health of her husband but not before she had appointed James Gardner as co-ordinator for the whole design.

James Gardner (he had designed the successful 'Britain Can Make It' exhibition at the end of the war) was 60 and had become a scholarship student at Chiswick School of Art at the age of 12! His remit was to balance the design of the ship and his main responsibility lay with the aesthetics of the liner's external appearance.

Because of Gardner's other work commitments, Dennis Lennon became joint co-ordinator and together they gave the *QE2* a balance of design. Everything was to be attractive but practical. There would not be one 'gimmick' on the ship and the two men would work closely with Dan Wallace, Cunard's naval architect, whose own team designed the structural layout of the ship often considering the needs of the interior designers in their work. The design team came from Britain, Canada and Australia.

From the earliest days of the Q4's construction, highly detailed mock-ups of various cabins had been built in the shipyard and these were constantly visited by design team members and many changes were affected. Passengers preferred beds to bunks

A designer's sketch of the captain's cabin. *University of Liverpool, Cunard Archives*

'Real' wood was used in several areas on the liner, such as in passenger furniture and decorative veneers and this photograph shows the Signal Deck being laid with teak planking. *Architectural Press*

Fitting out alongside the jetty at John Brown's Clydebank shipyard. Here the funnel had already been fitted. *George Gardner*

Above: A view of the Double Room, looking forward, from the top of the sweeping stainless steel and glass stairway. In later refits, amongst other changes, the upper lounge (the Double Up) would be given over as an extension of the shopping services.
University of Liverpool, Cunard Archives

Left: One of the majority of cabins that have a porthole. Compact and comfortable - luxury at sea available to everyone.
University of Liverpool, Cunard Archives.

Below: The space-age circular midships lobby. This would act as a lounge during voyages but would be the first class reception area whilst in harbour.
University of Liverpool, Cunard Archives

Part of the main kitchen on Quarter Deck as built. This kitchen would serve the Britannia Restaurant on the Upper Deck above it, the Columbia Restaurant aft on the same deck level as the kitchen and the Grill Room.   *University of Liverpool, Cunard Archives*

and a great proportion of the rooms (the word 'cabin' was dropped) were so fitted. Bath and showers were fitted more widely in rooms than ever before.

Because of the advanced planning of the rooms about ninety had been completed on board by the time the ship was launched.

During the building of the liner it was decided – after much difference of opinion – that a two-class ship would be more advantageous than a three class vessel (especially for conversion to cruising when she would become, to all intents and purposes, a one class ship). The existence of the mock-up cabins ensured that no real difficulties occurred because of this change of direction. The opportunity to change to two classes arose when delays in the building occurred: Cunard turned these to their advantage. One major disadvantage of the delays was that the 1968 Summer season on the North Atlantic would be lost.

Extra space was also made available by the resultant reduction in the number of public rooms and associated services. By one brilliant stroke two lounges (tourist and cabin) on adjacent decks were made into one, two decks high, with the upper lounge providing a lounge balcony overlooking the lower. The two decks were connected with a stainless steel and glass stairway, cascading from one deck level to the next. This brilliant joining of the two lounges became the 20,000 square foot Double Room, one of the largest rooms afloat.

Two restaurants instead of three, and one kitchen to serve both, were to be raised from the traditional position of such rooms

in earlier ships. The Verandah Grills in the earlier *Queens* had been popular, even in rough weather, because they were high in the ship and had large windows with sea-views. The other restaurants on the older ships were sited low down in the hull in order to reduce motion during stormy weather; (but they still remained un-patronised in such condition).

It was therefore decided to raise the restaurants in the *QE2* to the superstructure. The use of aluminium and the installation of stabilisers during building enabled the extra weight to be carried higher in the ship and both rooms were extended to the ship's side. Large windows built near to deck level gave wonderful views of the sea.

The kitchen, too, was raised for easy access to the restaurants, one aft and the other on the deck directly above the kitchen. Large windows were not needed in the kitchen so portholes were retained. One problem was noted by Jim Jone as he looked over the ship, as so many Cunard sea-going personnel did, to offer the benefit of his experience. In the *Mary* and the *Elizabeth* the kitchens, being low in those ships, had a garbage shute which opened to the sea through the bottom of the ship and down which rubbish could be jettisoned. There was no such shute on the *QE2* so garbage would have to be bagged and manually thrown overboard. That is, until a special door was cut into the side of the ship, disguised behind the large 'U' of the red CUNARD logo painted on the superstructure at the fore end of Quarter Deck.

One of the most elegant rooms afloat. Michael Inchbald's 'Queens Room' was decorated in white and silver and could be used for a variety of purposes.
Philip Rentell

Many of the layouts of public rooms and cabins had been created by the carefully selected group of designers with their designs co-ordinated by James Gardner and Dennis Lennon.

Some remarkably pleasant rooms were created and many designs were discarded along the way. Natural lighting was to be used as far as possible to take advantage of the large windows. The public rooms could be extended to the ship's side at night by utilizing what would be promenade space during the day.

As James Gardner was busy with the exterior styling of the ship Dennis Lennon carried on with some of the interior designs. Amongst his work were the Britannia Restaurant, the Queen's Grill (the successor to the popular Verandah Grills on the previous *Queen* liners where, on the payment of a supplement, passengers could enjoy an exclusivity denied to other passengers), the Theatre Bar (in shades of red) and the Midship's Bar (dark, mostly in greens).

The enormous Double Room (the balcony known as the Double Up, the lower deck the Double Down) was created by Jon Bannenberg and decorated with a red carpet and plum coloured suede walls. Bannenberg also did the Card Room in various greens and the swimming pool, on Six Deck, with its round changing rooms.

The classic Queen's Rooms, one of the most beautiful rooms ever to go to sea with its trumpet like columns, was finished in white and silver with a walnut veneered wall at one end which looked more substantial than suggested by its construction. A bust of the Queen, by Oscar Nemon, was set into a recess in this wall. Carpets and curtains gave a splash of colour in reds, honey and lemon patterns. Its designer, Michael Inchbald, also designed the Quarter Deck library, furnished with chairs of green leather, brown tweed sofas and other chairs of black hide and brass.

Don Wallace, Cunard's naval architect, designed the Midships Lobby with its twenty-six foot diameter recess. This lobby with its dark blue leather walls, would act as a reception area in port and as a lounge whilst at sea. Curved green sofas bordered the recess.

The superb 500-seat theatre could also be used as a conference hall or as a church as well as a cinema. Gaby Schreiber wanted different moods to suit different occasions by varying the colour of the lighting. She also designed several of the delux suites.

Some of these original rooms have long since disappeared, their spaces being used for other functions. Amongst those lost were two night clubs.

The first, the Q4 Room, was designed by David Hicks, the son-in-law of Earl Mountbatten of Burma. The walls were of grey flannel and as a night club the tables had black cloths laid on them in the evening. In the day time, however, the room could be put to other uses and the table cloths were changed to ones of red and pink, providing a brighter mood.

The other night club, the 736 Room, was the creation of Stefan Buzas who also designed the London Gallery. The 736 Room could also be changed from its night time purpose and become a bar and discotheque during the day.

Theo Crosby's Observation Bar (also known as the Look Out), with its forward views of the sea, was panelled in cedar veneer. This was the only public room with such a view and has now sadly been put to another use and denied to passengers.

Amongst many other works of art on board three tapestries that faced the entrance of the Columbia Restaurant were noteworthy. These depicted the building and launch of the *QE2* and were designed by the Canadian, Helen Banynina.

Statues, model ships, paintings and many other works of art would decorate the ship. The crockery and glassware, with its special *QE2* logo, was also carefully chosen and soon became targets for souvenir hunters.

Amidst all this luxury and comfort the safety of her future passengers had not been forgotten and was ensured by many lifesaving and safety features.

There were twenty ship's boats, placed ten on either side of the liner. Two class 'A' 27-foot emergency boats, painted red, were located at the fore ends of the boat deck. Four class 'B' motor launches and eight class 'B' lifeboats were all 36 feet long; the six 40-foot cruise launches could take sixty people ashore or act as lifeboats for 80 if necessary.

Sixty-two Beaufort inflatable life rafts could each take 25 persons. In all, the life saving equipment could accommodate well above the complement of the liner. 3,200 Hart-Imco life jackets were also provided.

The fireproofing of the liner also featured strongly in the technical press.

Cunard had been given a choice of either adopting the American method of using as little inflammable material as possible or the British concept of supplying adequate water sprinklers and an inert gas smothering system where electrical and other water sensitive equipment was in use. They opted to use both.

To comply with the acceptance of the American regulations a reduction in the use of natural woods was implemented, although the use of this most comfortable of mediums still appeared to figure strongly in the decor and furnishing of passenger areas.

This was done by using thin 1.5mm veneers of natural wood fixed onto backings of compressed, asbestos-based sheeting called 'Marinite'. Real wood furniture was also used, especially in passenger rooms.

In all 2,000,000 square feet of 'Marinite' was used on board the ship and it was often faced with wood or plastic. The Formica company produced several patterns of textured decorative laminates, all of which had been specially designed by the designers of the various rooms and these were bonded to the 'Marinite'.

The perilous effects of working with asbestos were just beginning to be recognized and the legislation that was being introduced to protect those shaping the material had to be fully complied with.

The joiners' unions had a field day and the management found themselves with a major headache.

The 'Marinite' was produced in 8 × 4 feet sheets which were delivered to a specially fitted-out part of the joiners' workshop. The cutting and drilling machines were fitted with vacuum extractors and the men issued with protective clothing. Those working the 'Marinite' were also sent for regular and frequent chest x-rays. Off-cuts and dust from the material were carefully gathered, bagged and buried in a disused quarry on the outskirts of Glasgow. This procedure was carried out once a week.

To double the shipbuilder's responsibilities towards the health and safety of its workers a similar procedure had to be carried out on board the ship where the material was often necessarily cut for final fitting.

Sometimes even after the panelling had been fitted it had to be taken down for further work to be carried out on the systems

concealed behind it. Usually, being fragile, it broke and had to be replaced. The workmen did not mind — it was continuing employment for them as it prolonged the job which, in turn, contributed to the delay in completing the ship.

'Marinite' was used as a fireproof ceiling too. Instead of being hidden by 'Formica' it was concealed beneath ribbed and polished aluminium or cedar planking.

As in many work places where 'attractive' items are being used a certain amount of pilferage occurred. This is called 'squirreling' on the Clyde and the *QE2* proved vulnerable to it.

To the shipyard the amount of 'squirreling' that took place was normal but to the Cunard staff seconded to the ship it was worrying. 'They are stealing an entire ocean liner and there is very little we can do about it', police officers told Chief Officer Bob Arnott.

Brass porthole fittings found ready exchange for a pint of the local ale in the pubs of Clydebank and Glasgow; short lengths of copper piping (often cut into length even after being installed on the ship) were easily smuggled out of the yard. One local house was raided and was found to be furnished almost entirely in 'squirreled' *QE2* material!

Light bulbs, light fittings, curtains, equipment from lifeboats, almost everything was marketable.

One of the worst cases was shown to a bedroom steward who had travelled north to view his new domain. The first class

Even with two 36-foot motor launches in place on the starboard side, the *QE2* is still far from complete. Note the small radial crane temporarily fitted aft on the Upper Deck. *Scottish Record Office*

HRH Prince Charles joined the *QE2* for her short trip down the Clyde from the shipyard to the drydock. Prince Charles is seen talking to Captain Bil Warwick and Sir Basil Smallpeice.

University of Liverpool, Cunard Archives

QE2, arranged for the ship to be opened to the public of Clydebank during the evenings. A long standing tradition would thus be maintained. (Similar 'open-evenings' were also held later at Greenock.)

One of hundreds who visited the liner, Lilian Gibson, remembers that a specific route around the ship had been laid out. This was not only for the visitors to admire the spaciousness and vastness (as well as noting the occasional incompleteness) of the ship but it was also for the benefit of the shipyard who wanted to steer their guests away from the unfinished areas which were 'a shambles'.

Visitors were still coming to the ship on the eve of departure and a namesake of the shipyard, John (T.) Brown, recalls joiners and other tradesmen still working in the passenger cabins in an effort to get as much 'work completed as possible. It seemed to him that 'there was still a long way to go'.

By 8 o'clock on the morning of 19th November 1968 Prince Charles was on board the *QE2* as she was readied for her first and final departure from the town that had brought her into being. A special holiday had been declared for the local townsfolk.

From the cold, dark, early hours of the morning great crowds had travelled by all means of transport to line the fields

Watched by thousands who had waited patiently in the early morning chill, the *QE2* sedately leaves her birthplace shortly after 8 am on 19th November 1968.

John T. Brown

reception area, the Midships Lobby, had been fitted with a beautiful carpet. It was there one evening at the end of the day shift: the next morning a large square of it had disappeared – cut out of the centre of the round recessed area. 'We won't come here again' a dismayed Cunard manager, referring to the yard, told the bedroom steward as they walked away from the scene.

Still, in spite of these irritations the *Queen* was fitted with £3 million worth of luxury. More irritatingly her completion date was put back.

To hurry the yard along Cunard announced that His Royal Highness Prince Charles would be at Clydebank to sail with the liner on the short journey down river to Greenock. Here, at Inchgreen, the *QE2* would be dry-docked to have the remains of her launch gear removed and to have her bottom plates cleaned and painted.

For the week before departure John Rannie, now Upper Clyde Shipbuilder's Clydebank director in direct charge of the

and shores alongside the River Clyde. Between Clydebank and Greenock an air of excitement and expectancy hung in the fresh morning air as each person patiently waited to watch the regal procession of the new gleaming liner.

John T. Brown came to watch the spectacle as he had done so on other departures. But he felt that the *QE2* was something special, and he brought along his cine camera, as well as his ordinary one, to record the event.

Captain Warwick was on board his brand new charge as she progressed down the river. He allowed the youthful Prince Charles the thrill of sounding the *QE2's* siren for the first time as the liner left Clydebank.

HRH had also been given a guided tour of the ship but, like the visitors before him, had been steered away from the unfinished areas.

The *Queen* passed round the bend at Dalmuir where the *Queen Mary*, caught by the breeze 35 years earlier, slewed round

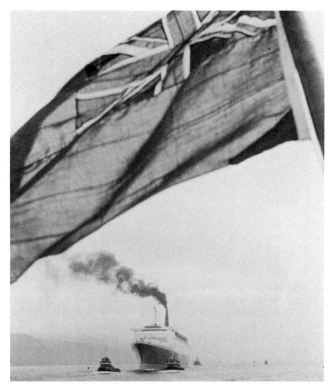

Accompanied by her tugs, the *QE2* steams down the Clyde and to the start of her trials. *University of Liverpool, Cunard Archives*

Once at Greenock she was carefully inched into the dry-dock and would remain there for a week, having work and inspections carried out on her underwater hull. Her rudder, internally, was maintenance free. Unlike her mighty antecedents, which had doors in their rudders for maintenance access, hers was filled with plastic foam.

The *QE2* was several months behind schedule but Cunard still hoped to have her ready for the lucrative summer season of the following year and had arranged a series of 'mini-maiden' voyages in the form of short cruises to prelude her maiden voyage proper to New York.

Each day hundreds of workmen were transported to Greenock from Glasgow and Clydebank to work on the unfinished cabins at the fore end of the ship. Feeding these men was a mammoth task but a local catering firm, who specialised in providing a service for ships going on trials, managed most efficiently.

She was due to sail on a comprehensive trial to the tropics, testing amongst other things, her air conditioning. But firstly, technical trials had to be carried out in the Irish Sea.

So, on 26th November she left Greenock for these preliminary trials which would allow a normal working-up procedure of the gearing. She achieved 164 revolutions per minute.

On 29th November the beloved *Lizzie* sailed from Southampton en-route for Florida, eventual re-sale three years later and ultimate destruction in the far-off waters of Hong Kong. The *Queen Elizabeth the Second* was the successor to a glorious precedent.

The following day, the 30th, the trials of the *QE2* finished unexpectedly. Oil fuel had contaminated the steam and feed system via the oil burner supply system and the liner had to return to Greenock. She was again dry-docked for a lengthy cleaning and decontamination period.

Her main trials to the Canaries were postponed. She had been due to sail on 4th December but, because of the unwanted extra work, this was postponed.

Cleaning completed, she left for a second trial on 17th December, finishing on the 20th. Speed had been increased to 177 r.p.m. and her full potential of 110,000 s.h.p. had been developed. She was vibration free and a new sailing date for her main trials was set for the 23rd.

Everybody was happy.

and had grounded for a few seconds, completely blocking the Clyde and causing great concern, and earning herself a place in Lloyd's daily casualty list!

Bob Arnott, later to become captain of the *Queen*, was on board as her first-ever chief officer and, as such, had been 'standing by' the liner since just after her launch. He now stood aft, in charge of the mooring lines and tow ropes.

The *Queen Elizabeth 2* steamed 10 miles down the river at a speed of around 6 knots leaving a Clydebank suddenly made empty by her departure.

As she left Clydebank John T. Brown caught a bus and raced to Greenock. He was fortunate enough to arrive in time to witness the liner's arrival there.

Off the Scottish island of Arran, the *Queen* was put through her paces. Her bulbous bow enabled her to achieve a creditable 29 knots without the tell-tale white bow wave that was usual when the old *Queens* were travelling at speed. *University of Liverpool, Cunard Archives*

Chapter Six

Trials and Triumph

By the end of 1968 prospects had begun to look brighter for Cunard as the grievous losses of previous years turned into profit. But this was only after complex and careful husbandry of financial resources and what Commodore Marr later described as 'the sale of Cunard'. By the end of the 'rescue' of Cunard only two ships were left at sea with Q4 on the stocks.

With fewer ships to operate, employees on shore as well as at sea had found themselves without a job, the unfortunate casualties of a hard-won victory. An especially bitter pill to swallow after, in many cases, years of loyal service to the company.

QE2, the symbol in steel of Cunard's retreat from the precipice of collapse, had had her main sea trials postponed until Monday 23rd December. The company then had to quickly arrange for some of its employees to act as guinea-pigs (less colourfully known as 'stiffs' to the crew!) for the trip. The first of the 'mini-maiden voyages' that had been scheduled for the new ship was to have been a Christmas charity cruise in aid of Cancer Research. As this was cancelled due to the delay in the completion of the ship a generous contribution would be later made to the charity by Cunard.

Hurriedly, Christmases were rearranged in many households as five-hundred passengers, consisting of employees and their families, headed towards Greenock.

The trials were to be sea trials in every sense of the word and the passengers had been instructed to order anything from the menus in order to test the kitchens and the ship's novel hotel department.

This was to help 'hone-up' the organisation on board as the trial was intended to be a dress rehearsal for the liner's commercial debut, a mini-maiden voyage to be taken as a cruise due to start on 10th January 1969. This in turn, would be a prelude to the maiden voyage proper leaving Southampton on the 17th for New York. A fourth 'maiden-voyage' was also scheduled for 1st February, leaving New York for the West Indies – an early test of the fabulous liner's duel-role.

Many of the crew had transferred to the new ship from the *Queen Elizabeth* and travelled north to Scotland on a freezing overnight train. These circumstances gave some of them a foreboding for the future.

On trials off the Scottish coast, the *QE2* performed superbly. She is seen here executing a turning circle.

University of Liverpool, Cunard Archives

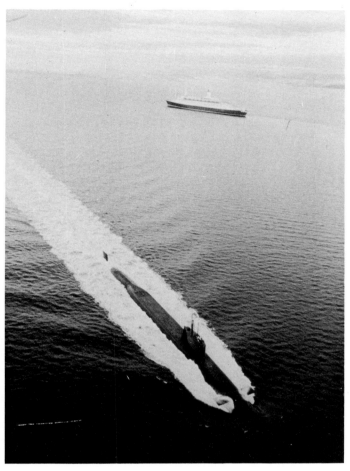

Two fine examples of Britain's maritime engineering: one built for peace, the other for defence. *QE2* passes a 'Resolution' class nuclear powered submarine. *University of Liverpool, Cunard Archives*

Because the new *Queen* would be away from Britain for long periods of time during cruises, the crew found that they had been given neat, two-berthed cabins instead of the old dormitory style rooms that had held from twelve to twenty men. Their new dining arrangements also ensured that they would not have to eat almost where they stood as had been the case in the past. The officers also found themselves in tastefully decorated rooms.

The provisions of smaller rooms for the crew was all very pleasant but it would eventually help to destroy the sense of community (that had come from the occupancy of the old dormitories) and which had induced such fierce pride in individual ships.

The standard of food, too, was altered. Surprisingly though, the standard of choice but not of quality for the men went, if anything, down! This was at the men's own instigation, their opinions being represented by chief steward Jimmy Smith. In the old ships the stewards, for example, had to eat what the passengers were offered; but it was all very well having superb roasts, steak, fowl, etc for dinner every day but that, it was pointed out, was not how the men ate when at home. How about steak and kidney pudding, tripe and onions or Irish stew? Home cooking was what was wanted. The company concurred.

Novel design was the hallmark of the *QE2* and this extended to the hotel staff's uniforms. Stewards were given beige jackets ('like a bush jacket!') and white polo neck jumpers. Some expected to find 'The Thoughts of Chairman Mao' tucked away

in the breast pocket! The new uniforms looked smart and were fine if the wearer was slim, but worn on torsos that were sometimes over fond of food or perhaps a few pints of good English Ale the new design 'looked . . . awful', as one bedroom steward put it. The uniforms would be changed within a year.

The new hotel organisation on board the *QE2* caused other problems for the crew. In the past passengers were served with tea and biscuits in their cabin before going for breakfast in the main restaurants; but now they could order breakfast in their rooms. This meant a double trip to a cabin: one to pick up a checked off breakfast menu and another to deliver the meal. Twice the walking!

Most of the 'teething problems' caused by the new concepts were soon sorted out at staff level but a more serious problem would soon be facing the ship herself.

For the shake-down cruise to the Canaries the shipyard had embarked two-hundred men. Mainly consisting of joiners, plumbers and electricians as well as shipyard and engineering workshop staff, it was hoped that they could complete the unfinished work in the cabins at the fore end of the ship. Upper Clyde Shipbuilder's (Clydebank) director in charge of the *QE2*, John Rannie, embarked with his wife.

Far from luxuriating in their surroundings the passengers had to earn their keep. There was still a lot of cleaning and washing down of walls to be done and the embarked Cunard staff set-to to do what they could to get the liner ship-shape.

All was going well until ten o'clock on Tuesday 24th December – Christmas Eve.

Down in the Turbine Room a small-bore pipe on a pressure gauge sited over the starboard h.p. turbine fractured, spilling oil over the ahead and astern turbine, and over the differential expansion indicator which then gave a warning, apparently due to flooding with oil.

At the same time vibration was noticed to be coming from the turbine and it was at first thought that this was due to the cold oil that was being spilt onto a hot part of the machinery.

Speed was reduced on the starboard engine as an attempt was made to account for the continuing vibration.

By 3.35 in the afternoon the vibration increased severely and the turbine was stopped. The port engine was slowed to 60 r.p.m.

The starboard h.p. turbine was inspected and this examination continued until 8.30 on Christmas morning. Two hours later the starboard engine was re-started until both engines were achieving 150 r.p.m.

This speed was maintained until 4.15 on Boxing Day morning when the errant turbine once again started to vibrate. Reduce speed was ordered once more until, twenty-four hours later, the turbine was stopped altogether and allowed to cool. Just before breakfast the turbine was again started; the vibration was still there but it was not so strong as it had been.

The problems were far from over as it was now the turn of the port side machinery to malfunction. By the early evening the vibration had increased. At 8.30 on the morning of the 28th the bridge ordered speed to be reduced as the ship was approaching her anchorage off the Canary Isles where she stopped with engines on 'Stand by'.

Just after 5 o'clock that afternoon, the *QE2* weighed anchors to proceed to Las Palmas but, as she got underway, a bumping noise was heard coming from the starboard turbine followed by a grinding crunch. After this the turbine ran vibration free, the ship reaching Las Palmas three hours later where she anchored at 8.25pm.

Immediately on anchoring Sir Basil Smallpeice and Anthony Hepper came on board having previously flown out from the UK. A meeting that would last for eight hours was then held in the Card Room with Tom Kameen, Cunard's technical director, reporting that John Brown Engineering did not yet know what had caused the damage let alone how to cure it.

Angus Gibson, one of the John Brown tradesmen on board, wrote home from Las Palmas: 'There has been trouble with the engines for the past two days. I don't think we will be getting ashore. We are only stopping for a couple of hours. The weather is quite good but not a lot of sunshine. We are working most of the time so there is not much time for relaxing. There is not much to do anyway except go to the pictures. If all goes well we should be docking at Southampton on Wednesday 1st January . . .'

The letter posted on board the *QE2* bore an ironic 'Acceptance Trials' cancellation mark.

Sir Basil Smallpeice kept the ship's company informed of events over the tannoy. Members of the press had also embarked at Las Palmas and they now sent, fortunately, mostly sympathetic and often enthusiastic reports home.

That evening John Rannie spoke to his men at dinner and asked them if they would be willing to work for another seven days at Southampton after their arrival there.

On the following day, Saturday, 'J.R.' sent a radio message to his shipyard manager, Boyd Haining, telling him that a turbine had broken down and that the ship was at anchor. The fault was major and could not be rectified at sea. To bring the ship back to the Clyde was just not practical: Southampton was the nearest suitable port.

Boyd Haining was also instructed to contact Geoffrey Moss, managing director of Cammel Laird's at Birkenhead, with a view to leasing their submarine/trials accommodation ship the *Cammel Laird*.

The shipyard manager was invited to inspect the vessel and his heart sank when he subsequently saw the result of many months of neglect. However, Geoffrey Moss recalled some men from their Christmas holidays and the vessel, the ex-Irish Sea ferry *Royal Ulsterman*, was made habitable. The *Cammel Laird* tied up at the Ocean Terminal at Southampton a day and a half

before the great Cunarder arrived at her new home for the first time (which was also her port of registration). (All the other great Cunarder's had been registered at Liverpool although they had used Southampton for many years.)

It took *QE2* three days to limp home, arriving in Southampton on January 2nd, one day later than had been anticipated. Sadly, the day before, a ship's hotel officer, George Boyle, had collapsed and died.

The planned reception for the ship that had been organised by Cunard was cancelled as the company said that it would not be 'the splendid arrival it should have been'. A launch to carry officials; hundreds of inflated balloons; the Hampshire Police Band; all were cancelled.

However, the Sotonians felt differently and they warmly welcomed 'their' new ship that would replace the former *Queens* in their hearts. The Mayor and other city officials welcomed the ship on behalf of the city and a feeling of celebration pervaded the ship and town.

John Rannie slipped quietly ashore, returning to Clydebank to complete the paperwork for the ship's completion and handing over. He was not to board the liner again for many years.

As Boyd Haining reached the top of the gang-way he was greeted by Bert Farrimond, personnel director of UCS, with the words: 'Now I know how Mafeking felt'! Boyd Haining's first job – he was responsible for personnel matters for the Clydebank division as well as being shipyard manager – was to pacify the Scottish workforce and to get their problems sorted out.

The 'Bankies' were eager to get home and many were still suffering from 'having celebrated rather too well over the festive season' (Hogmanay having occurred a few hours previously). The secretaries on board could not cope with the clamour for travel warrants or for money, hence the greeting given to the personnel manager on his arrival.

Over the next few days the situation was eased, as the workmen went home on leave and fresh men arrived from Scotland. On their arrival they found that accommodation had been arranged for them around the city; the *Cammel Laird* had

Captain 'Bil' Warwick surveys the river ahead of his liner as he takes her to sea for the first time. *Architectural Press*

met with initial disapproval as being too cramped, especially after the men now on leave had experienced the luxury of the *QE2* whilst on trials. Berthing on the smaller vessel was later reduced by half.

More men were also flown down from UCS (Clydebank) as the turbine breakdown had provided an ideal opportunity to at last finish the uncompleted cabins. The engineering difficulties thus proved to be 'an enormous blessing in disguise' for the ship-building department as all publicity now fell on the turbine troubles and attention was diverted from the unfinished state of the accommodation.

Vosper Thornycroft sent in local squads of platers, welders and caulkers to assist with the work and daily meetings were held between shop stewards of both shipyards presided over by the shipyard manager of UCS. Fourteen-hundred men were soon to be working on the liner.

Daily meetings were also held between Cunard (headed by Sir Basil Smallpeice) and Upper Clyde Shipbuilders, represented by Tony Hepper and John Brown's technical director, John Stark.

Cunard had refused to accept the ship of course and at one time even considered selling her. Sir Basil even put forward ideas that, whilst laid-up, the ship should be hired out for private functions to help make her pay.

Relations between the two companies became increasingly strained; at one point they became so strained that Cunard decided to withdraw the facility of providing lunch time coffee and sandwiches for all staff. The shipping company had just cause to be angry. All sailings (six altogether, losing £2 million) had had to be cancelled starting with the maiden voyage, and an expensive advertising and marketing campaign written off. The crew, so painstakingly trained, had to be retained throughout the repair period and many were sent home on full pay.

By this time many heated debates had taken place in the House of Commons. David Price, Member of Parliament for the Southampton district of Eastleigh, made a plea on January 24th: 'At this moment the clear priority is for the *QE2* to be completed successfully and speedily and nothing should be said or done that would divert those concerned from fulfilling that purpose'.

During the early part of January the immediate priority of repairing the damaged turbines had been put in hand. On the *QE2's* arrival in Southampton the covers had been removed and the turbines visually inspected.

The immediately visual evidence of damage to the starboard turbine was that hundreds of blades had been stripped from the main body of the rotor hub. A complete circle of blades at No. 9 stage and several from stage 10 had been carried away and lay at the base of the casing. On further inspection cracking could be seen at the bases, or roots, of other blades. In the starboard turbine the damage was less extensive, seven blades had gone from stage 9 and there was some cracking in stages 8 and 10.

The rotors were taken out, boxed and flown back to John Brown Engineering Ltd. on 6th January, leaving the turbine room looking like 'a flour mill' after the insulated cladding had been stripped off.

A thorough investigation to assess the causes of the damage and to make recommendations that would obviate their re-occurrence was set in motion. The investigating team worked under the leadership of Sir Arnold Lindley, President of the Institute of Mechanical Engineers, and their findings were published in an important paper (by Messrs. Coats and Fleeting) that was read to the Institute of Marine Engineers.

It was found that the blade roots, which were square, did not expand as much as could be expected and that the steam supply nozzles, used to deliver steam on to the blades, were of below standard quality. There were also too many of these nozzles.

The badly damaged starboard high-pressure turbine rotor. The extent of the damage to the 9th and 10th stages of blades can be clearly seen.
Shipbuilding and Shipping Record

The resultant vibration and resonances that were induced in the blades proved to be too much and as one cracked and sheared it took away its immediate neighbour until masses of blades had been torn from the rotor.

The remedy was to provide new blades with strengthened roots and to 'tie' them together with a continuous length of one eighth of an inch stainless steel wire welded between all blades of each stage, thus providing a stiffness and a resistance to resonance.

Sir Basil Smallpeice thought that such a basic fault that had caused the damage should have been found during test-bed trials and blamed John Brown Engineering. Pametrada, the turbine's designers, had gone out of business under the Geddes committee recommendations that had streamlined so much of Britain's shipbuilding and marine engineering industry.

The port turbine rotor arrived back at Southampton by road and arrived at Vospers for inspection on the evening of Saturday 1st March.

With the arrival of the starboard rotor imminent, Sir Basil Smallpeice announced that the maiden voyage of the *QE2* was scheduled for 2nd May with proving trials first taking place, and there was no foreseeable reason why Cunard should not take delivery by the second half of April. He said that by then her accommodation would be 100% complete and there would be no doubt about the reliability of her engines: 'QE2 will more than fulfil the promises made to her prospective passengers as to her performance.' He added: 'She will be the most superb example of the shipbuilders craft the world has yet seen.' Taking another chance to market the liner Sir Basil finished: 'QE2 is certainly a new place to visit between New York and London or Paris!'

The North Atlantic was almost finished as a highway between Europe and the USA. During January there was only one sailing from Southampton by a transatlantic liner. The German *Bremen* of North German Lloyd had the windfall of taking the passengers originally intended for the *QE2's* postponed maiden voyage of 17th January. She had also picked up the passengers who should have sailed on the now strike-bound *United States* – the holder of the out-moded Blue Ribband – the fastest liner that the world had seen.

Cunard's vision of a ship for all seasons was about to be vindicated.

A typical study of the *QE2* in the Ocean Dock, Southampton, alongside the now demolished Ocean Terminal.   *Norman Jackman*

Photograph amidst the splendour of a Norwegian fjord, the *QE2* sports the light blue anti-fouling paint that she wore for only a few months. The paint has a self-polishing property that helps to reduce fuel bills by cutting down resistance.   *Cunard*

Above and below: The first arrival of the *QE2* in Southampton was far from the splendid arrival it should have been as the ship limped in at slow speed. Fortunately the press was sympathetic.   *Both, R. Bruce Grice*

Chapter Seven

The Best

The refurbished turbines were reinstalled and the ship-builders assured Cunard that the liner would be completed two weeks ahead of the revised estimated schedule.

When all was ready in the engine room, QE2 was put through her basin trials. These consisted of various engine trials undertaken whilst the liner was tied up alongside the Ocean Terminal. To test the reliability of the main machinery overspeed tests were carried out which involved the disconnection of the propeller shafts from the engines and running the latter at higher speeds than could be expected in the normal operation of the ship.

The basin trials were happily successful. The next test would be to take the ship on a short series of trials in the English Channel, off the southern coast of Hampshire and Dorset.

So, after three months delay, at 7 o'clock in the evening of Monday 24th March the QE2 sailed at last leaving Southampton for the first time, under the command of Captain Warwick and with Jack Holt on board as pilot. Amongst those on board were two men with a keen interest in the outcome of the short sea-trials – Sir George Gardiner, chairman of John Brown Engineering and Sir Arnold Lindley, President of the Institute of Mechanical Engineers. They were looking forward to the tests with 'cautious optimism'.

The liner anchored for the night off the Nab light-tower in the eastern approaches to Spithead and the next day compass trials were undertaken. A speed of 18 knots was also achieved.

The 'swingiest fashion show ever staged' took place on board whilst the liner was underway and five-hundred press-men were embarked to record events.

As the passengers sat down to lunch the American superliner *United States* sailed by. As she did so one man was reported, perhaps apocryphally, as saying: 'There goes the world's fastest liner.' His companion came back with 'but not the best'! The latter's retort would soon be echoed by many.

Anchoring each evening off the coast the QE2 was put through full speed trials during the day. She also did a crash stop in which she came to halt in seven minutes, travelling one-and-a-half miles in doing so. Going astern she reached a speed of fourteen knots, sustaining this speed for a lengthy period.

Back in Southampton on the 27th the QE2 entered the King George V dry dock in the Western (also known as the New) Docks at 7.30 in the evening. It was the building of this very dock, the largest in the world when it was opened in 1933, that had finally persuaded Cunard to use Southampton as its British terminus for the *Queen Mary* when she was being built.

Unusually it would be from the flooded dry-dock that the new *Queen* would sail on her previously interrupted shakedown cruise to the tropics to test her air-conditioning.

During the day of 30th March seven-hundred invited passengers boarded the liner; in the early evening several members of the hotel staff walked off the ship. They were protesting about what they felt was excessive vibration in about ten cabins on Five Deck caused when the liner was travelling at her normal service speed of 28 knots.

The company promised to investigate the complaint (two months later, after further complaints, the worst affected cabins were turned into staff offices whilst others were fitted with extra insulation) and the crew re-boarded the liner. The *Queen* sailed at 9.30pm.

During the first few days of April the *Queen Elizabeth 2* proved her worth. Her passengers were more than happy with both their accommodation and the service. The engines – especially the turbines – performed superbly. Averaging a speed of 30 knots the liner, on occasion, reached more than 32.5 knots.

After reaching the coast of Senegal at about 15° latitude north of the Equator (where the passengers stayed cool in their air-conditioned paradise whilst the air temperature outside reached 90°F) the liner turned north to steam around the Canary Islands before heading once again for Southampton. She arrived back in the port on the 7th.

The next day Sir Basil Smallpeice held a press conference and declared himself 'highly satisfied' with the liner. Although she had lost an estimated £3 million because of her unhappy start,

The sheer grace of the liner's forward hull can be judged from this quayside photograph, taken as the ship safely reached Southampton after her disastrous trials. *University of Liverpool, Cunard Archives*

Slowly edged into her berth, the new *Queen* prepares for many weeks of battling between owner's and builders.   *R. Bruce Grice*

Sir Basil stated 'she is being handed over to us in a better condition than I ever thought possible at one time'.

Sir Arnold Lindley was also happy with the remedial work that had been carried out on the turbines: 'I think we can regard the trouble with the turbines now as something in the past', but Upper Clyde Shipbuilders wanted to satisfy themselves that this was so. They announced that they were hoping to hand the ship over to Cunard on the 18th of the month but would first open up the turbine casings for a final inspection.

At a private lunch on board on the 14th April Sir Basil Smallpeice, his deputy chairman Lord Mancroft, Cunard's managing director John Whitworth and Anthony Hepper, chairman of UCS, entertained three-hundred VIPs including the top civic dignitaries of Southampton; representatives of the port, shipping and commercial interests; the lone, world circumnavigating yachtsman Sir Alec and his wife Lady Rose; and the last captains of the two great deposed *Queens* – Geoffrey Marr and John Treasure Jones.

It was announced that Her Majesty Queen Elizabeth II would visit the liner that she had launched twenty months earlier on the day before the maiden voyage proper, May 1st.

As previously stated the liner was to be handed over to the Cunard Line by her builders on Friday 18th March, but the official ceremony did not take place on board the ship: Unusually it took place in an office many miles away in London and occurred one hour later than originally announced.

At the same time, 1.15pm, in Southampton, the liner gave a three blast greeting on her whistle as the builder's flag was lowered and the scarlet flag of Cunard with its rampant golden lion clutching a globe was raised in its place.

The ship, at long last, belonged to Cunard.

A captain of *QE2* talks with a captain of industry. Bil Warwick chats with Sir Basil Smallpeice, the one man to whom Cunard would owe its survival.   *University of Liverpool, Cunard Archives*

Chapter Eight

Royal Approval

The *Queen Elizabeth 2* was due to depart on her first voyage with fare-paying passengers, leaving Southampton on Tuesday 22nd April 1969. This would be in the form of a short cruise to Las Palmas in the Canary Islands, and was billed as the first 'mini maiden voyage' of the new liner.

Amongst the hundreds of activities taking place that would prepare the liner for her commercial debut was the consecration of the shipboard Jewish Synagogue, designed by Professor Mischa Black, and performed by Chief Rabbi Dr Jakobovits. Professor Black had declined the offer of utilising the old synagogue of the *Queen Mary* in the new ship as he considered the *Mary's* synagogue as being 'not in keeping with the modern trends of the Jewish faith'.

At 4.45 in the afternoon of the appointed day, the *Queen* sailed to the sounds of a military bank playing on the quayside as a mass of balloons was released. Hundreds of spectators watched as the liner was gently eased in Southampton Water by tugs gaily dressed overall with flags that stiffly fluttered in the prevailing gusty wind.

The cruise would last eight days and in its course would encompass the discovery and disembarkation (to a pilot cutter) of a stowaway, the christening of little James Clifton and the death of a fifty-one year old male passenger.

Arriving back in Southampton on Wednesday 30th April, the liner was prepared for her Royal visitors who would be inspecting the ship the next day. Her Majesty the Queen would be following the royal precedents set by her grandmother and mother when they had visited their mighty namesakes on the eves of their maiden voyages.

The Queen and the Duke of Edinburgh duly arrived the next morning at 11.50 am and stayed on board for two and a half hours, touring the ship with Captain William Warwick and Staff Captain George Smith who acted as guides.

Amongst the many fittings in which the Queen showed great interest were the navigational aids on the bridge. She also admired a figurehead of Britannia (the name of Samuel Cunard's first pioneer transatlantic paddle steamer) in the Britannia Restaurant. The figure, carved in yellow pine, had been presented by Lloyds of London. This 'wooden maiden' had lost her fingertips after a particularly lively party on board a few weeks earlier!

Lunch was taken in the Grill Room with the guests sitting at tables of four. The Queen sat with the captain, Sir Basil Smallpeice and the Vice-Lieutenant of Hampshire, Lord Malmesbury, lunching on melon ball cocktails, cold Avon salmon, mayonnaise, new potatoes and a green salad; strawberries and cream followed; a 1962 Montrachet was served. The Queen would later compliment the executive chef, Mr Townshend, on the meal and its serving.

After lunch the royal party walked through the lovely Queen's Room (this room had been flooded with oil during fitting out; an act of vandalism, it was rumoured, to delay the final departure from the Clyde). Lord Mancroft, Cunard's chief of marketing, pointed out to Her Majesty the bust of herself sculpted by Oscar Nemon. Although it was only a painted plaster cast, the Queen was interested to see it in the position that the actual casting would finally occupy.

Sir Basil Smallpeice recalled the conversation: 'You are putting it here, are you?' the Queen asked, 'How did he manage to finish it so soon?', Lord Mancroft explained that it was only a plaster copy. The Queen then described her seven sittings for the sculptor and how each time Oscar Nemon had been dissatisfied with his work. The Queen continued, quoting Nemon: 'That's no good' he says, and wrenches my head off!' whereupon the Queen twisted a clawed hand above a clenched fist to give demonstration of the sculptor's action, much to the delight of onlookers.

Before she left the ship the Queen remarked about the excellent condition of the vessel and expressed her hope for a happy maiden voyage that would be starting on the following day, and for a subsequently successful career for the liner.

The euphoria of the royal visit was replaced the next day by that of the QE2's departure for New York on her long delayed maiden voyage. The original maiden voyage to New York, that should have started on the 17th January, would have taken a circuitous route taking thirteen days via the Canaries and the Caribbean; a mixture of cruise and North Atlantic ferry voyage combining the two roles that had been designed into the ship.

Rain in the morning had failed to dampen the excitement that prevailed in Southampton and many vantage points both within and outside of the docks were occupied by people in their thousands.

Fourteen hundred passengers had been booked for this premier voyage; some people were only taking the short channel

The Oscar Nemon bust of Her Majesty Queen Elizabeth II which adorns a small alcove at the forward end of the lovely Queen's Room. The bust was altered in colouring from copper green to gold during a recent refit.
Philip Rentell

A very dismal 2nd May 1969 witnessed the *Queen's* maiden departure for New York. A good crowd still attended the event. *Southern Newspapers*

trip, but six hundred others were making the complete round voyage, obviously considering that the chance to attend this party-of-a-lifetime was too good to miss! The ship also carried nine hundred and six crew in all departments.

The liner had been scheduled to leave the Ocean Terminal at 12.30, but because of a delay caused by the handling of the baggage she was a quarter of an hour late in getting away.

The Hampshire Police Band had entertained the crowd of well-wishers on the quayside as well as those lining the railings of the liner's boat deck but, as she pulled away, trumpeters from the band of the Royal Corps of Transport played a specially composed fanfare 'Cunard Queen'.

Hundreds of brightly coloured balloons bespeckled the sky as Buccaneer jets of the Fleet Air Arm flew overhead. Arms waved as the thin paper streamers thrown from the high decks of the liner broke, the last tenuous link between ship and shore.

A bevy of small craft awaited the liner in the main stream, and tugs used their fire-fighting equipment to send plumes of water high into the air in joyous salute.

A little later as the *QE2* passed the jetties at the Fawley oil refinery, the tankers berthed there added their throaty greetings. The *Queen* responded with her siren.

Turning to port off Cowes on the Isle of Wight – always a vantage point from which to watch the comings and goings of the great liners – the *QE2* headed towards Le Havre, her next port of call.

The French harbour was delighted at being chosen as the European port of call for the new Cunarder. Up until now Cherbourg had had the honour of serving the previous *Queen's*

and a huge crowd had turned out to greet her as she docked on schedule.

The liner was handled through the agencies of the French Line (Compagnie General Transatlantique) as Cunard had since closed its own agency in France. It was a nice extension to the co-operation that would exist between the *France* and the *QE2*. It was also actually CGT who had given preference to Le Havre on behalf of Cunard.

During the two hours that the liner stayed in Le Havre one hundred passengers disembarked to return to the UK, the European passengers embarked and then the *Queen* was off – destination New York.

The maiden voyage was unhappily marred by the death of a sixty-one year old steward, 'Jack' Sharp, and his remains were committed to the sea as the liner came to a temporary halt in mid-Atlantic.

New York had prepared a welcome to outdo the departure from Southampton. Mayor John Lindsay had declared 7th May, as *'Queen Elizabeth the Second* Day' and, with a group of civic dignitaries, boarded the liner in the Lower Bay.

Bathed in sunshine and escorted ahead by the US Coast Guard cutter (which had brought out the mayor and his party) and a US destroyer astern, the *Queen* sedately approached the famous Manhatten skyline, the water around her continually churned white by the accompanying fleet of pleasure craft, tugs and river ferries.

Bob Arnott recalled a patriotic thrill derived from 'a gigantic sea and air display of twin triumphs in British design, advanced technology and engineering skills' when a 'jump-jet

Greeted by an enthusiastic crowd, (which would become typical all over the world as the Queen took to cruising), the liner arrives at Southampton assisted by tugs.   *Architectural Press*

(Harrier) hovered at each extremity of the bridge as we entered the harbour'. This surge of patriotism would find a home in many British hearts in the years to come when the ship would be welcomed in many foreign ports.

The *QE2* docked at Cunard's New York terminus, Pier 92, in the North River at just after 3 pm.

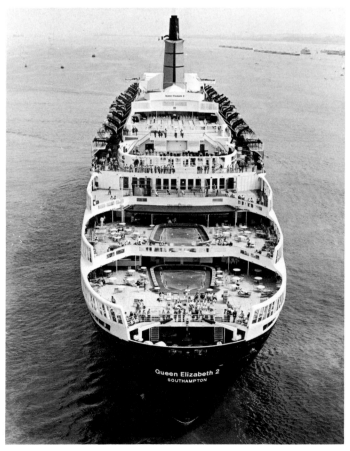

The after decks of the *QE2* provided a cascading sun trap for the passengers. Each of the aluminium framed verandah windows had been individually manufactured to suit the bevel and sheer of the ship's lines. These decks would be changed to suit a variety of purposes in future years.
                                                                    Cunard

The City's Mayor, John Lindsay, said that the ship would 'continue the Cunard tradition of sailing great ships into this, the greatest port in the world, for decades to come'. Thousands of people were entertained on board the new ship as she became the 'in' place in New York with socialites and politicians of many countries counted amongst the guests enjoying the British hospitality.

The New Yorkers, like the Sotonians in Britain, had been surprised at the *QE2's* appearance. Her all enclosed superstructure gave away the comforts of an air-conditioned interior, but the funnel was the strikingly different feature of the ship. Gone was the traditional Cunard funnel of carmine red with two or three narrow horizontal black bands and a broad black top; in its place was a device that was almost a sculpture. A black pipe, protruding from a white casing, surmounted a soot and smoke deflecting windscoop that was white on the outside but painted in 'Cunard red' on the inside. The terraced decks aft of the funnel cascaded to the stern providing both shelter and sun trap; the hull itself also broke from the traditional black, being painted in charcoal grey to the contemporary British Standard of BS-9-028.

The company shade of red was also echoed in the name of CUNARD painted on either side of the forward superstructure. Deck-house sides along the boat deck, and also the bridge front, had been painted in light khaki to give additional depth. In the styling of the liner's exterior, James Gardner had done his job well.

Visitors on board were also surprised at the spaciousness of the vessel. Compared to the space allotted to each passenger on the old *Queens* each passenger now had fifty per cent more deck area. Combined with her modern decor the liner presented an almost revolutionary appearance; she was a superb blend of good and practical design.

Counted amongst the twelve hundred passengers on the return leg of this, the first voyage, was one of the principle guests at the official New York reception, Lord Louis Mountbatten.

A few days after her arrival back in Southampton Lord Louis sent an autographed photograph of himself to the officers' wardroom to 'update' the one of himself that had graced a similar position in the old *Queen Elizabeth*.

With a total complement of 2,025 the *Queen's* early voyages were somewhat underbooked, but that was put down to the season. West bound traffic was particularly under-patronised in the early days for, when the *QE2* returned to Southampton, she was scheduled to carry only seven hundred on the next trip to New York.

Amongst these were two well known personalities. The Southampton newspaper, the 'Echo', reported Peter Sellers as saying, 'it's nice to have the time to take a little rest on board. You get a little tired jetting it everywhere'.

As almost an accolade to the modern image of the *QE2* Ringo Starr, the drummer of the phenomenally popular music group the 'Beatles', was also travelling: 'It's rather like a splendid hotel – better than you get at Scarborough!'

The *Queen* sailed on her second westbound voyage on Friday 16th May, at 12.30 pm.

Outward bound through Spithead she passed through the assembled, multi-national fleet of NATO which the Queen was reviewing (making it an unique occasion as reigning British monarchs had only ever reviewed British fleets) from the Royal Yacht *Britannia*.

The liner blew her loyal greeting as she drew abreast of the Royal Yacht, Captain Warwick signalled: 'Captain Warwick and the ship's company of the *Queen Elizabeth 2* with their humble duty send their best wishes and hope that Her Majesty will have an enjoyable day reviewing the NATO Fleet'.

The after verandah decks provided a sheltered meeting place - weather permitting.   *Architectural Press*

A group of celebrities boarded the liner for her delayed trial cruise to Dakar and the Canaries.   *University of Liverpool, Cunard Archives*

Her Majesty replied: 'I am grateful for your signal. I send you and all on board my best wishes. Bon voyage. Elizabeth R.'

The Royal interest in the liner was continued on the ship's next arrival in Southampton. On Thursday 29th May His Royal Highness Prince Philip Duke of Edinburgh paid a lone visit to the ship to present awards on behalf of the Council of Industrial Design.

Many weeks earlier when it was suggested that the awards should be presented in surroundings that epitomised the spirit of the occasion the Duke himself suggested the *QE2*.

Gaby Schreiber's theatre was chosen as the venue for the presentation of the eighteen trophies. The Duke toured the liner visiting passenger and crew areas, as well as control rooms and kitchens. He backed up his selection of venue by saying that '. . . the ship represented the culmination of the work of a great many designers in a great many fields'.

Throughout the summer of 1969 the *QE2* showed her paces and proved her worth. It would, it was realised, take time to make an impression on the source of her main market, the Americans, but meanwhile the liner put Cunard back into the realms of viability.

She proved herself worthy of the faith that had been so painstakingly placed in her. In the first six months of operation between her maiden voyage and the end of her eleventh round voyage in September, she realized a profit of £1,674,000. The plug in the drain on Cunard's resources had become a foundation on which to build for the future.

Chapter Nine

Serenity, Security and Storm

To relate each and every voyage of the *QE2* and to chronicle every incident that has befallen the liner would be beyond the capabilities of this book.

However, be it sufficient to say that the *Queen*, like so many other ships before her, usually remains out of the news as long as she performs what is asked of her: the quiet and efficient performance of her scheduled voyaging.

Safe navigation and the careful maintenance of her fiercely demanding timetable has ensured that the liner has continued the Cunard Line's enviable reputation of never losing a life during peacetime operations.

Incidents are bound to happen, of course, when a ship – such as the *QE2* – annually sails so many thousands of miles. It is usually the occurrence of such incidents that brings the *QE2* into the headlines but often these events are a result of outside influences or because of accidents happening to other vessels in which the Cunarder becomes involved, through her responding to calls for assistance.

Sea lanes, like their land-based counterparts, are safe so long as their users observe specific laws and rules. Imprudent navigation on the part of other ships may, on the rare occasion, put the *QE2's* navigators to the test, especially at the 'junctions' of popular cruise ports where ships of many flags converge – sometimes too speedily!

Like most highways, those of the sea can occasionally produce a sudden drama and one ship may call on another to assist her in her distress.

The big chance of the *QE2* came on 8th January 1972.

Whilst cruising in the Caribbean the French Line's handsome *Antilles*, white hulled with the company's deep red funnel with its black top, was sailing in the vicinity of the island of Mustique, the passengers being given a closer look at the scenery.

In spite of frantic warnings from local inhabitants the ship sailed in rather too closely and struck an uncharted reef. Her oil tanks ruptured and oil spilled into the surrounding tropical seas and, worst of all, into the liner's own engine room where it ignited.

Soon the liner was ablaze and the six hundred and thirty five people on board gave the vessel up to the flames and abandoned ship. One of the ships within capable reach of the stricken *Antilles* was the *QE2*, herself on a cruise to the exotic islands of the Caribbean. Still under the command of Bil Warwick, the liner weighed anchor from her stopover point in St. Lucia and sped towards the scene of disaster.

On arriving at the location at 10.30 pm, the *Queen* found the night sky lit in a pulsating dome of dull red by the blazing French vessel. By now the *Antilles* passengers had been transferred to the island by their ships boats and it was from here that the *QE2* picked up over three hundred survivors. Initially it was thought that many had perished but these people had been picked up by other ships from another local island.

QE2 sailed at 5.30 am and later landed her rescued at Barbados. Amongst the many messages of congratulation that Captain Warwick received was one forwarded by Cunard from the President of Compagnie General Transatlantique (the French Line) and passed on to the ship by an equally grateful Sir Basil Smallpeice: 'I want to thank you for the assistance which has been afforded to us by Cunard in the accident which struck our liner *Antilles*. Please convey to the captain of the *QE2* our deep appreciation for taking onboard passengers which our crew had evacuated and put on Mustique Island.'

Fire is the most feared of all the fates that can befall a ship at sea. For centuries many fine ships – including such maritime jewels as the *Henri Grace À Dieu* of Henry VIII, Charles I's carved and gilded *Sovereign of the Seas* and the impeccable *Normandie* – have blazed to total ruin and ways had been sought to at least control, if not obviate, the fiery nightmare that might occur.

The *QE2* had been built to be as fire-proof a ship as possible, at the time of building conforming not only to current and potential British legislation but also to American. Fire-resistant materials and superior automatic fire extinguishing and detection equipment make the *Queen* one of the safest ships to have been built. Trained fire patrols in harbour or dry-dock ensure that the unhappy fate that befell the beautiful *Normandie* does not reoccur.

Even so, the liner has not been entirely immune from fire but these have been quickly and efficiently dealt with.

A particular engine room blaze in 1976 left the *Queen* without the use of one boiler and she limped back into Southampton with the lower white casing of her statuesque funnel blackened. The effected boiler had to be replaced by dry-docking the liner by cutting an access hole in her side to remove the damaged machinery and install its replacement. Similar damage to an

The external evidence of the blaze in which one crew member was injured in 1976.   *Southern Newspapers*

older ship would, perhaps, have resulted in its premature scrapping.

Fire when unchecked, can destroy even the best of Man's creations whether afloat or on land but the main cause of wanton and deliberate destruction is often Man himself.

One occasion arose during the eventful early years of the *QE2's* career and was one which would seriously affect the liner's future security arrangements – including her public accessability.

It all began in New York, May 1972. Of many evening classes being held at various locations in that bustlingly cosmopolitan city was one particular English class at Hunter College in Manhatten. A pupil of the class, Miss Barbara Shelvey, had written a short story based on a shipboard bomb scare of a previous year and Miss Shelvey's own uneventful voyage on the *QE2*.

The action of her story took place on board the Cunarder and involved two main characters who had booked passage. One character was a Mrs. Garth, terminally ill with cancer, and the other an ex-convict who found no joy in life. Their plan was to hijack the liner by holding-up the captain on the bridge at gun point and then commit a jewel robbery prior to escaping in one of the ship's launches.

Because of Miss Shalvey's shyness the evening class teacher, Professor Philip Freund, read the short story to the rest of the class. Only five students were present in the class that evening and one remarked on Miss Shalvey's 'fantastic imagination'.

A few hours after the reading a telephone call was received at Cunard's New York office, taken by Charles Dixon, Vice President finance and operations of the company's American organisation.

The caller said that unless a ransom of $350,000 was paid in ten and twenty dollar bills two accomplices, one terminally ill with cancer, and at that moment on board the *QE2*, would detonate six explosive devices, depth charges, concealed within the ship.

The FBI was called and Cunard alerted the Ministry of Defence and Scotland Yard in London. Money was obtained with which to pay the ransom in New York whilst, in England, the RAF readied two aircraft: a Hercules which would fly out a bomb disposal team and a second aircraft, a Nimrod, which would be used for communications.

The military bomb-disposal team consisted of four men – Captain Robert Williams, Sergeant Clifford Oliver, Lieutenant Richard Clifford and Corporal Thomas Jones. Together the men represented the Special Air Service (SAS) and the Special Boat Service (SBS) of the Royal Marines.

The liner had been en-route for Cherbourg (the *QE2* had reverted to using this traditional Cunard port instead of Le Havre in early May) and Southampton, but had hove-to in mid-Atlantic to embark the military parachutists. On board for Voyage 84 were 1,438 passengers including the conductor, Leopold Stokowski, and Mr George Kelly, Uncle of Princess Grace of Monaco. It was May 18th.

Captain William Law had previously arranged a search of the ship and informed the passengers of what was happening. Generally they remained calm, but one or two women, who could not apparently stand the suspense, were visibly upset.

Excited passengers lined the ship's rails to watch as the four parachutists appeared, dropping from beneath the low cloud base into the sea at the liner's starboard bow. A ship's launch under the new command of Junior First Officer Robin Woodall (later to be a captain of Cunard's Caribbean cruise-ships and later relief Captain of the *QE2*) picked up the men and brought them to the ship. After the first officer had introduced their leader, Captain Williams, to Captain Law on the bridge the army com-

mander reached inside his wetsuit and produced a copy of that day's newspaper which he presented to an astonished skipper.

The military men then conducted a search of strategic points in the passenger accommodation, baggage storage rooms etc.

About an hour after the disposal team had boarded the rumours started: 'They have found two bombs already in Two Deck baggage area!', a stewardess excitedly told crew-member Barney Gallagher and his work-mate.

The bomb scare proved, as was suspected, to be without foundation and nothing was found.

The Manhattan evening class professor had, by now, heard the news of the bomb scare and realized the close similarity between his pupil's story and fact. He telephoned the police and the next day a New York show salesman, Joseph Lindisi, was arrested. He was later sentenced to twenty years imprisonment pending a psychiatric examination.

Although the whole affair had been a hoax Cunard had gained valuable first hand experience in anti-terrorist security, and ship-board security was subsequently tightened. No longer would the casual visitor be able to stroll around the ship whilst in port – and out went the traditional 'Bon Voyage' parties held by passengers in their cabins for those friends being left behind.

But as one very relieved American passenger said after the dramatic mid-Atlantic meeting between ship and security forces: 'It was very comforting to think that Britain can still reach out.'

Although deliberately induced harm has been guarded against (more than it had been in the air) the ship is, as are most types of transport, still prone to the whims of nature.

'WNA' is a marking on a vessel's load-line which indicates a special condition: Winter North Atlantic. The designers of the *QE2* did away with winter on the North Atlantic for their ship as it was planned that the ship should go cruising during this inhospitable Atlantic season. Although the *QE2* can still encounter storms on this ocean information given by modern navigational aids and computers can enable the bad weather –

May 1972 saw British military parachutists jumping into the sea near a stopped *QE2*. A bomb hoax had started a full-scale exercise which still has its echoes in the continuing security arrangements today. *Cunard*

and sometimes, in early Spring, ice – to be avoided by sailing around the affected area.

But when inclement weather is unavoidable then the force of the sea, which man can only ignore at his peril, can often leave its mark.

In April 1972, the month before the bomb hoax, one particularly severe storm lasted for several days and the *Queen* arrived in Southampton 36 hours late.

The six hundred passengers were presented with bouquets upon disembarking, leaving behind them pianos, crockery and glassware smashed by the effects of the turbulent ocean.

Captain Mortimer Hehir also presented a signed 'Storm Certificate' to everyone on board:

This is to record that on her North Atlantic voyage leaving New York on the 16 April 1972, for Southampton, England, *RMS Queen Elizabeth 2*, of 65,863 gross tons encountered exceptionally severe weather in position Latitude 42° 18′ North, Longitude 55° 52′ West.

During this storm, winds reached speeds in excess of 100 mph. Combined with heavy swell, waves were encountered of 50 feet in height.

This weather caused even the *Queen Elizabeth 2*, with her exceptional size and sea-keeping qualities, to lie hove to for 21½ hours between 17th and 19th April 1972, until the storm abated.

I commend all passengers in sharing this unique experience with great cheerfulness and calm.'

Mortimer Hehir
Captain

The 'uniqueness' of this particular storm was spoilt in September 1978, when Captain Douglas Ridley encountered similar severe weather which damaged the liner's fore peak railings.

The ship's size and ability to weather most seas was proven when the liner went to the rescue of a yacht, crippled in a Mediterranean storm during the season of the Mistral.

A northerly gale was blowing on 25th September 1974 when, as the *QE2* cut her way through the heavy swell of the

---

QUEEN ELIZABETH 2

STORM CERTIFICATE

This is to record that on her North Atlantic voyage, leaving New York on the 16th April 1972, for Southampton, England, RMS QUEEN ELIZABETH 2, of 65,863 gross tons, encountered exceptionally severe weather in position Latitude 42°18′ North, Longitude 55°52′ West.

During this storm, winds reached speeds in excess of 100mph. Combined with a heavy swell, waves were encountered of 50 feet in height.

This weather caused even the QUEEN ELIZABETH 2, with her exceptional size and sea-keeping qualities, to lie hove to for 21½ hours between 17th and 19th April 1972, until the storm abated.

I commend all passengers in sharing this unique experience with great cheerfulness and calm.

Mortimer Hehir.
Captain

An early spring crossing of the *QE2* in April 1972 met a late severe gale. The captain had this special certificate issued to commemorate the event. Passengers were also given bouquets as they disembarked.

T.S. Gough

Mediterranean between Naples and Barcelona, distress rockets were seen at 3 am. Responding promptly to the call for help and in order to avoid causing further damage to the French yacht *Stephanie*, which was in immediate danger of sinking, Captain Peter Jackson stopped his liner some way off and allowed her to drift over to the stricken vessel, thus giving her a lee in which the six survivors could be rescued from almost certain death. The flare that the captain had seen had been their last but one.

The liner then gave warning of the wreckage to other ships in the area and the next day the US cruiser *Little Rock* of the US 6th Fleet confirmed that they had sunk the remains of the yacht.

Peter Jackson was later received by the Chairman of Lloyds of London in recognition of his masterly navigation and humanity. From other authorities came silence, a strange reward indeed for such a notable action.

Danger lurks not only on the surface of the sea but also under it, waiting for the unaware navigator.

The *QE2* had gone to the rescue when an unchartered reef had caused the total constructive loss of the *Antilles* and it would be, ironically, an incorrectly chartered reef that would cause enough damage to the *QE2* to warrant her dry docking for repairs.

This happened during a Caribbean cruise when the liner was manoeuvring in the 'swinging' ground at Nassau prior to sailing. As the liner's bow turned, her underwater bulbous bow collided with a coral reef, was holed and the liner had to proceed to New York, the remainder of the cruise being cancelled.

Captain Hehir was held responsible but on the 28th January 1976, the liner's next call at the port, Staff Captain Peter Jackson, along with first Officers Sturge and Warwick and members of the ship's sub-aqua diving club took a boat and set off to investigate the reef.

To the exoneration of their captain they found, by the use of sextant readings and landmarks, that the reef had been incorrectly charted: instead of running practically straight it had two 50 foot 'headlands' and on one of these, which projected from the charted line, was found evidence of the *QE2's* collision. A marker buoy was also found to be incorrectly moored (being 130 feet away from its recorded position) and the two errors combined confounded the ship's navigators' assumption that the safe water that they had reason to expect was not there.

It is usually the *Queen's* involvement in dramatic events that ensure her of a headline and general public interest, but to the thousands who travel on the *QE2* it is the trouble-free ferry voyages across the Atlantic or her cruising to places of interest that evoke the happy memory of ports visited and sights seen.

Her winter cruising days started with forays to the Caribbean from New York but, by 1975, these had developed into full World Cruising. The *QE2* has now completed either one of these cruises or else a comprehensive Pacific cruise each year and many new and exotic ports have been added to her itinerary for the delight of her passengers.

She broke new ground for Western liners by cruising to China in 1975. On her popular visits to Hong Kong the *Queen* often takes advantage of an economic cosmetic treatment when local painters swarm over bamboo scaffolding, erected precariously on small boats bobbing around the ship, giving her hull a smart new coat of paint.

The liner's transition of the Panama Canal is always popular, with passengers crowding the rails to witness the event. The largest ship to pass through the canal, the *QE2* also pays the highest fees but the savings in fuel costs by doing so far outweighs the longer passage south. However, the *QE2* is due to round the Horn in a special South American cruise in 1989 following in the wake of the *Queen Mary* when she passed Cape Horn en route to her final destination at Long Beach in 1967.

Attended by 'mules' on the rail tracks to either side of the lock, the *QE2's* 105-foot beam (still in her post-Falklands livery) is eased through the lock-gates whilst transiting the Panama Canal. (Her maiden passage through the canal was in 1979). An expensive journey of a few hours cuts out an even more expensive alternative voyage of rounding the Horn.   *Captain Borland courtesy of Southampton City Museums*

From Southampton the liner cruises to the Atlantic Isles, the Iberian Peninsula and to the Mediterranean. North Cape cruises, too, are extremely popular with the liner dwarfed by the magnificently spectacular scenery of the Norwegian Fjords as she steams in sheltered deep water between sheer mountain cliffs, cascading with pine forests and waterfalls.

During the course of the *QE2's* World Cruises her passengers have many options open to them. One of these is to join the ship for only part of the voyage and the experiences gained from such a journey can be most enriching. Owing to the cessation of the majority of the old-style, regular liner voyages a part of the *Queen's* cruise can be used as a substitute, making a visit to friends or relations that much more rewarding. Passengers can join *QE2* anywhere in the world by plane and in recent years the ship has enjoyed a unique distinction in being paired with that superb product of Anglo French co-operation, Concorde.

The list of islands visited in the Pacific – Tonga, Tahiti, Fiji, the Society Islands where one can see fish swimming in the coral from glass-bottomed boats – seems endless. Dancing to Joe Loss and other bands, discos, midnight buffets, patriotic departures from New Zealand and the gala firework welcomes in Australia (which make the British amongst the passengers proud to be British) all make world cruising in the *QE2* so popular with many people often repeating their bookings. Wry British humour on board, whilst appreciated by compatriots – 'Watch out for the bump!' as the liner crosses the Equator – can leave other passengers worried!

During one Pacific cruise of the *Queen* in the early 1980s, Alan Whicker, the television presenter of 'Whickers World', based one of his series around the liner. This proved to be very unpopular with the crew as it encroached on their private relaxation and gave, perhaps, a one-sided view of life on board – and on shore. Many people, including passengers, refused to take part in the glossy documentary.

The *Queen Elizabeth 2* is an extremely popular visitor to Japan, her arrivals there drawing crowds to the quayside numbered in thousands. Yokohama, especially, gives the liner a rapturous welcome, so much so that the city has chartered – at a reported fee of £14 million, the ship for 'Yokohama Exotic Showcase '89' which will commemorate the 130th Anniversary of the Port and the centenary of the municipality of the city. The charter will extend from March until September 1989 and will last for seventy-two days.

One particular charter was surrounded by a extraordinarily high-level of security that was, fortunately, never brought into action.

The *Queen Elizabeth 2* sailed not only into New York, in early April 1973, from a Caribbean Cruise but into the start of an intense security exercise.

The liner had been chartered by Assured Travel of Worcester, Massachusetts, run by Mr Oscar Rudnik. He had conceived the idea of chartering the *QE2* to take travellers to Israel to join in the celebrations of the Twenty Fifth Anniversary of that State's founding.

Cunard had anticipated carrying twelve hundred passengers each way but that would turn out to be the final total number for the entire voyage. Mr Rudnik had hoped to recoup his subsequent losses by using the liner as an hotel whilst she was in Israel,

Above. The *QE2* at anchor in one of the many exotic harbours that she visits during the course of her annual cruising itinary. Originally the liner had three anchors at the bow: one each side, port and starboard and a stem anchor just below the forepeak on the bow. This anchor became lodged in its hawsepipe in an Atlantic storm early on in her cruise and was subsequently removed. *Cunard*

Left: Leaving New York in the early 1980s, this photograph shows the build-up of penthouses on the Signal Deck just behind the bridge. *Cunard* but permission to do so was refused by the Israeli government.

However, the *QE2* sailed into an even tighter security net when she arrived in Southampton on April 11th. Her dock was sealed off, passes were required and scrutinised and frogmen patrolled the water around the stationary liner. Lorries were searched as they delivered stores.

Captain William Law went on sick leave with a strained back and his relief captain, Mortimer Hehir, took over. The crew each demanded £50 danger money for the voyage plus four years wages should they fall victim to Arab terrorists during the voyage.

Questions were asked in Parliament ('Who was paying for the Civil and Military security?' 'Cunard.') and the passengers (mostly American Jews who had saved for this 'trip of a lifetime') arrived in Southampton in coaches accompanied by police escorts. Fifteen men with Israeli passports reportedly boarded the ship at Southampton as did members of the SAS who would keep a low profile during the voyage guarding strategic points, such as the bridge, and keeping their conversation to the minimum with the crew with whom they came into contact. Ten members of the crew having Irish connections were put ashore in fear that they might identify the SAS men to unfriendly Irish agents. Cunard's own security people reportedly placed dummy bomb-like objects at various points around the ship which, using a percussion cap, made a loud bang if moved. The astute crew found and reported each device and, as instructed, not one of the devices was touched.

Crowds once again lined the shores of Southampton Water as the *QE2* sailed on Sunday 15th April.

Her next port of call was Lisbon in Portugal. The security conscious Portuguese closed the Salazar Bridge whilst the *Queen* passed beneath it and the security surrounding Rochas Quay reflected the Portuguese watch against hi-jacking, ever intense since their own liner, the *Santa Maria*, was taken over by an anti-governmental faction several years before.

Sailing on, the *QE2* passed through the Straits of Gibraltar. Here, the fabrications that emmanated from the media during this 'non-event' of a danger cruise were in evidence. A radio reporter, broadcasting 'live', described naval craft coming out from 'Gib' and steaming in line ahead and astern of the liner in glorious sunshine. The ship's radio officer, listening to this report, went on deck. The 'glorious sunshine' was murk and nothing could be seen of the navy! Unhappily, this standard of reporting existed throughout the cruise and dismayed many of the crew.

The liner passed north of Malta and Crete thus avoiding the North African coast. This was done, the captain was reported as saying, to avoid the unintended provocation of the anti-Israeli North African Arab nations who might think that 'we are thumbing our noses at them'.

The liner sailed through most of the Mediterranean to Ashod in blackout. Her arrival at that port angered many Orthodox Jews as it occurred on a Saturday.

David Ben Gurion visited the ship before she left for Haifa, where she stayed for a few days, later returning to the new deep water berth at Ashod. Strict security surrounded the ship at all times with passes being thoroughly scrutinised both at the dock gate and at the ship; troops continuously patrolled the dockside and fast patrol craft were in evidence out in the open sea. Anti-personnel devices were detonated in the harbour at night around the floodlit ship in order to deter unfriendly divers.

The *Queen* spent just over two weeks in Israel before returning to Southampton, where the security exercise was repeated, on Sunday 13th May.

The whole charter may have passed into the realms of 'just another cruise' but for a startling revelation made one year later.

The late President Sadat of Egypt was being interviewed on the BBC television current affairs programme 'Panorama'. In it he said that he was awoken in the early hours one morning by a telephone call. The caller asked for confirmation of orders issued by President Gaddafi of Libya with whom Egypt was sharing a political and military alliance under a temporary unification of the two countries.

President Sadat rescinded the orders immediately when he found out what they were. Gaddafi had ordered an Egyptian submarine to go and sink the *QE2*!

The *QE2* once unwittingly aided the deadly aims of terrorism when, on October 20th, 1971, the liner called in at Cobh in Southern Ireland. After she had sailed, six suitcases were found unclaimed on the quayside and a burly Irishman attempted to lift them. Unable to do so because of their weight he alerted the authorities and subsequently a cache of arms intended for the IRA was discovered.

The story was continued three years later when, after a long police investigation, a gunfight took place in the unlikely setting of Southampton. It all ended with the arrest of Gabriel Megahey, a quiet Irishman, one time stevedore and Cunard crewman, – but the head of the IRA unit in the Hampshire city.

Adventure for the *QE2* there has been, but the great majority of her journeys are safe and happy voyages. Apart from charters – including one from New York to inaugurate the new deep water oil terminal at Come-by-Chance in Canada when John Rannie (the managing director of the ship's builders) travelled on the liner that he had built for the first time since her disastrous trials – the ship sails on special or inaugural trips to many ports that welcome her as an honoured guest. Some of these ports are subsequently used as frequent ports of call such as Boston which the liner visited for the first time in 1971.

The vessel was the centre of attention in her American home town of New York when, watched by millions, she opened the festivities surrounding the Hundredth Birthday celebrations of the Statue of Liberty in 1987.

In May 1982, the city of Philadelphia on the Delaware river welcomed the ship for the first time. (*QE2* has visited this port on many occasions since, including one arrival detoured from New York when, at the end of a special trip to celebrate the Fiftieth Anniversary of the *Queen Mary's* maiden voyage, she diverted there to avoid ice in the Atlantic).

The first visit was as part of the celebrations surrounding the city's 300th anniversary of its founding by William Penn. During her stay in the 'City of Brotherly Love' thousands of paying guests were entertained and fed on board the liner, helping to pay for the ship's stay there; the ship's restaurants ran an almost non-stop service.

The visit was a great success and many Philadelphians took the opportunity to sail with her back to Southampton.

It was during this voyage that the curtain rose on the most dramatic episode in the *QE2's* history.

The requirements of Cunard and peaceful commerce would soon be laid aside in favour of the needs of the *Queen's* country.

Chapter Ten

Echoes of War

'Often whole divisions at a time were moved by each ship. Vital decisions depended on their ability continuously to elude the enemy, and without their aid the day of victory must unquestionably have been postponed . . .' These words, written after the end of the Second World War by Winston Churchill, referred to the work done by the *Queen Mary* and *Queen Elizabeth* in safely transporting thousands upon thousands of Allied troops to the war zone. Towards the end of that conflict each ship was carrying fifteen thousand GI's on each trip from New York.

Churchill estimated that their joint contribution to the Allied effort shortened the war by at least a year.

No-one ever thought that Britain would have to call on the services of the last of the country's Atlantic liners to act in a similar capacity, but the unthinkable was about to become reality.

Captain Peter Jackson had been enjoying the last few days of his leave at his home near Southampton and was due to take the *QE2* over from his relief captain, Alex Hutcheson, for her next trip – a cruise to the Mediterranean.

It had been six weeks since the Argentinians had landed on South Georgia on Friday 19th March 1982, and almost a month since the Argentinian army had invaded the Falkland Islands, those specks of British Colonialism claimed by the Argentinians as their 'Malvinas'.

A week after the invasion the requisitioned Peninsular and Oriental liner *Canberra* had sailed south as a troopship, carrying 3 Commando Brigade, and it was 'on the cards' that the *QE2*

might also be called-up to join 'Operation Corporate'. But Cunard continued to scoff at any such idea.

So far Peter Jackson had received no word at his home that anything was about to happen to his ship, except that she was a little late and would not be berthing until about midnight. So it was with great surprise that the captain listened to the BBC One o'clock News on Monday 3rd May. The *QE2* had finally been requisitioned by HM Government to transport three thousand troops to the Falklands.

The news, too, came as a surprise to those on board the ship. Many heard the same BBC news that had surprised Captain Jackson, others remained in ignorance – including the relief captain, Alex Hutcheson! The first that he heard of the requisitioning was when the BBC telephoned him for confirmation.

First Officer Philip Rentell and some friends were on their way to lunch. Bumping into one of the liner's nursing staff they were asked if they had heard the news and their initial state of shock lasted throughout their lunchtime.

Just as the liner was approaching The Lizard, Captain Hutcheson made a broadcast to passengers and confirmed initial reports. As he finished, the sound of cheering could be heard coming from various parts of the ship.

The liner docked with her port side against the Queen Elizabeth II quay in Southampton at two minutes past midnight on the morning of 4th May, the passengers disembarking between 9 and 10.30 am after breakfast.

Following her call-up the Cunarder was quickly converted into Her Majesty's troopship *Queen Elizabeth 2*. Her forward heli-pad is here being fitted after previously being prefabricated by Vosper Thornycroft's shipyard.
Len Betts

One of *QE2's* officers studying the girder supports to the aft heli-pad sprouting from the after swimming pools, the area on the liner capable of supporting great weights.　　*Southern Newspapers*

Weighed down with luggage, troops of 1st Battalion, the 7th Duke of Wellington's Own Gurkha's Rifles prepare to board *QE2*.　　*Southern Newspapers*

4 pm Wednesday 12th May and *QE2* leaves Southampton carrying 3,000 troops of 5 Infantry Brigade.　　*Southern Newspapers*

By 8 o'clock that morning the Ministry of Defence was already at work. Chief Officer Ron Warwick (son of the *QE2's* first ever captain) and Phil Rentell accompanied a naval representative as the latter made quick decisions on how to turn the liner into an aircraft carrier. The ship's officers were horrified to hear him say 'oh yes, I think we can chop this lot off here', referring to the verandah windows aft, and also making a suggestion that the swimming pool should be filled with cement to take the weight of a forest of red-leaded, steel flight-deck supports which would bear the load of landing helicopters.

The upper aluminium superstructure, being constructed for lightness and maximum passenger use, was not sufficiently strong enough to take the weight of the proposed 'heli-pads' so the highest steel deck was chosen to take the feet of the new supports. Quarter Deck suited the bill and the heli-pads were eventually built level with the next highest deck, forward in front of the bridge-front hatch and aft level with One Deck.

Captain Jackson arrived on board at 10 am only to find his cabin already full of Cunard officials, including Executive Captain Douglas Ridley, and people from the Department of Trade, Lloyds and Royal Naval and military personnel.

That evening at 10 pm the liner was turned starboard side to the quay. It was not until 10.30 on the morning of Thursday 6th May, that an increasingly unhappy Captain Jackson heard via a 'phone call from Ralph Bahna, chairman of Cunard, that he would be actually sailing as Master of the *QE2*. As he was not in the Royal Naval Reserve the liner would continue to fly the Red Ensign of the Merchant Service, thus indicating that the ship was of a non-combatant status.

In turn the captain telephoned his wife to tell her the news. He now felt that he could get his teeth 'into this project with some enthusiasm'.

That day saw the start of the work to prepare the ship for her future role as the decks were stripped in the areas that would accommodate the heli-pads.

Much furniture, paintings, sculptures, ship models and fruit machines had already gone ashore along with stores, such as the caviar, that would not be required on the voyage. Military stores flowed in the opposite direction although ammunition would not be loaded until the 9th.

Meetings were held every day both on board and in London as the conversion was satisfactorily progressed. On Saturday 8th Captain Jackson took Ralph Bahna around the ship to show him the 'general devastation and new construction'. The captain considered his chairman to be 'in a state of shock for a while'!

Over the next few days the ship took on a more orderly appearance as she prepared to take on her hundreds of expected guests. Carpets which could not be taken ashore were covered in hardboard sheeting fixed together with black tape. The names of troops were later marked on the hardboard flooring outside the cabins that they were to occupy.

Workmen from Vosper Thornycroft's shipyard worked around the clock to get the ship ready. Prefabricated heli-pads that had been constructed in advance in the plate shops of the yard were now transported to the docks. Here they were lifted onto the liner and welded into place, huge table tops on many legs made of vertical 'I' bar girders.

First Officer Phil Rentell was also a lieutenant in the R.N.R. and, on the *QE2's* arrival in Southampton, had gone home to Sutton Coldfield to collect his uniform. He had volunteered for the Falklands trip and had been asked by Douglas Ridley, himself a senior officer in the R.N.R., to travel south acting as a liaison officer between the ship and the naval party.

A Royal Naval preparation party came on board on the eve of departure to ensure that everything was ready for the troops' embarkation the following day.

On the morning of sailing, Wednesday 12th May, Captain Jackson arrived on board early at 6.30 am only to find that troop embarkation had already started. A 'Heads of Department' meeting had been arranged for 9.15 am with Ralph Bahna and Bernard Crisp in attendance; at 10.30 am a navigation and flying operations briefing session was held on the bridge. Peter Jackson had already studied charts of the port to be visited en-route for oil and water (Freetown in Sierra Leone) and had decided that there would be a sufficient depth of water for the *QE2* to go alongside the QEII quay in the container terminal there.

As the morning melted into the afternoon troops that made up 5 Infantry Brigade still continued to ascend the gangways, entering into a world of barely concealed luxury that would be their barracks for the days to come.

Each of the units that boarded had a band or piper to play them aboard. The Gurkhas created the biggest stir – their priest blessing them as they boarded – weighed down with back-packs almost as big as the fearsome soldiers that bore them. The Gurkhas would be berthed low in the ship where they would be less vulnerable to the sea-sickness to which they were prone.

By early afternoon Royal Naval Party 1980, Headquarters Land Forces Falklands Islands and 5 Infantry Brigade were all on board, eagerly seeking their cabins or improvised dormitories before going back on deck to watch the excitement of departure.

A large crowd had gathered on the quayside and bands played cheerily. Television cameras relayed the occasion in complete contrast to the secrecy that surrounded the similar trooping movements of the *Queen Mary* and *Queen Eliabeth* to and from the Clyde during the Second World War.

The world knew where the *QE2* was going and what she was carrying. The world knew that Prime Minister Margaret Thatcher meant business!

It had seemed that all the top 'Brass' wanted to come to see both the ship and the troops before the departure and the quayside alongside the ship took on the appearance of a heli-port. Lord Victor Matthews, head of Trafalgar House, arrived on board at 12.30 am. The culmination to the flow of visitors came when John Nott, the British Minister of Defence, visited the ship, moving quickly amongst the troops so that he could not be asked any awkward questions.

Although the world outside was in a patriotically festive mood Captain Jackson had not yet had his share of worries for the day.

As the afternoon built up to a crescendo of fervour, the Captain received a message at 2 pm that all was not well in the engine room. One boiler had been shut down for maintenance, and now a second boiler had developed a massive leak in its supply of distilled water, 20 tons an hour, which could not be traced.

It was essential for publicity purposes that the ship should sail on time – even on the one boiler remaining in service. So, at 1545 hrs – with Captain Peter Driver on board as pilot, a force 4 to 5 wind blowing from the south east and with three tugs made fast forward and two aft – 'Stand By Engines' was rung on the ship's telegraph.

At 1603 hrs all mooring wires and ropes had been released and the liner headed up-river, there to turn in the stream before heading down towards the Isle of Wight.

Two tugs let-go by the Brambles buoy, two others let-go a little later leaving the little *Albert* alone at the bow to give the underpowered *Queen* extra manoeuvreability should she need it. She was achieving forty revolutions which gave her a speed of seven knots.

Around half past five, two 'Sea King' helicopters arrived, their pilots skilfully testing the turbulence created by the forward motion of the liner and landed on the after flight deck.

Using an improvised swimming pool made of wood and canvas on the forward heli-pad the troops celebrated the tradition of the 'Crossing of the Line' ceremony.   *Imperial War Museum*

The *Albert* released her charge at 6 pm as the *QE2* headed eastwards towards the Nab light tower.

Captain Driver disembarked onto the pilot launch at 8 pm just as the liner had the Nab on her starboard beam.

The *QE2* would anchor overnight 3 miles south of the Nab and away from the gaze of shore based sightseers. During her stay there the Admiralty tug *Bustler* came out from Portsmouth with various additional stores in the early hours of the morning.

At 8 am on Thursday Peter Jackson was advised by the engine room that the ship would be ready to sail at 9 am. The source of the distilled water leak had been detected: a valve had simply been left open! During the next hour all lifeboats were tested and swung out and the engines, too, were checked. At 9.20 the anchor was hauled up and, fifteen minutes later, the *QE2* was underway.

The troops were put through their first lifeboat drill. It proved to be quite chaotic but many lessons were learnt and subsequent drills proved to be more proficient. Because of the lower deck on which they were accommodated the Gurkhas would have to ascend several decks to their lifeboat stations. So, in case an emergency should take place and the ship was darkened, these Nepalese warriors practiced finding their way blindfolded!

Because of the vast distances to be travelled the *QE2* would need to have her oil supplies replenished at sea whilst underway. To this end an oil pipeline had been fitted on Two Deck which would take the oil to the tanks.

To practice the art of Replenishment-at-Sea (RAS-sing as it was colloquially known) the liner was due to redezvous with the Royal Fleet Auxiliary vessel *Grey Rover* later that afternoon.

Before then, however, two patients had to be flown off the ship by helicopter to the nearest hospital. As the liner was due south of The Lizard this happened to be Treliske Hospital in Truro, Cornwall. One patient had a torn Achilles tendon and the other had suspected appendicitis which turned out to be meningitis. Unfortunately this patient later died.

The huge Double Down Room became the troops' mess.   *Southern Newspapers*

Above: QE2 in Cumberland Bay, South Georgia, with the cross-decking of troops clearly in progress. The wintery conditions are very apparent in this rare colour view.
Captain Peter Jackson

Left: Only occasionally did a helicopter use the forward heli-pad. Trying to land at the same speed of the ship and having a 65,000 ton hotel approaching at 27 knots was a daunting prospect for many a helicopter pilot.
Captain Peter Jackson

However, the ship's nurse who accompanied the men, Jane Yelland, thoroughly enjoyed her flight and took the opportunity to relieve the hospital of as many newspapers that she could find for the benefit of the men on board the troopship *QE2*.

The *QE2* met with *Grey Rover* on schedule, a line was passed and in one minute a token ton of oil pumped from the tanker to the liner. The pipe was then blown through to clear it and the ships parted. The whole operation was a success and had only taken three quarters of an hour.

On the Friday, with the ship doing 24 knots on two boilers, Captain Jackson gave written instructions to the Chief Engineer for the passage to Freetown and Ascension. This would necessitate the use of all three boilers so efforts were increased to get the third boiler 'on-line'.

In the days that followed, the troops set themselves training tasks. Stripping down and reassembling small-arms, jogging around the deck – each unit had its own allocated time, and woe betide anyone who infringed it! – attending various lectures, or practicing firing small arms over the ship's side. Black garbage bags, full of rubbish and which were normally discharged at night,

Jokingly known as 'paraffin pigeons' to the ship's crew, the helicopters practiced using the heli-pads in readiness for *QE2's* arrival in South Georgia.   *Brian Atkinson*

After conducting the Sunday church services, Captain Peter Jackson (right) got himself 'fully booted and spurred' in flying kit and was taken on a flight around his ship.   *Courtesy of Captain Peter Jackson*

were thrown overboard and used as targets. Greater care had to be taken with live ammunition as the ship's officers complained that the railings were being shot through in several places!

The captain and officers swapped their blue uniforms for 'whites' on the 15th as the *Queen* approached warmer waters. Also, on this day, the third boiler was brought into action and so a good reserve of speed became available.

Helicopter exercises were carried on daily. After conducting the Church Service on the first Sunday at sea, Captain Jackson attired himself in full flying kit, joined a helicopter, and took the opportunity to take some photographs of his ship from the air and to investigate a Russian Intelligence Gathering Auxiliary 'posing as a trawler'. His verdict on the flight? – 'What a wonderful experience'!

During the captain's absence, his ship was technically (as well as physically!) without a master, so Peter Jackson officially handed over the command of the liner to his relief, Alex Hutcheson.

That evening the captain joined the Gurkhas for dinner. It was their eightieth birthday and he received a lethal Kukri as a gift.

Of the actual ship's crew six hundred and fifty had volunteered to go south. The stewards were told that they would not really be needed as the army units would provide their own messing arrangements. However, many stewards did go, some of them with experience from the previous war on board the old *Queens*, and served in the officers' messes.

The crew were later to be thanked by 5 Brigade's commanding officer, Brigadier Wilson, when he said that both he and his troops had the greatest respect for them. They (the crew), he said, had volunteered whereas he and the troops had had to go to the war zone. It was, after all, their job.

At 8 am on the 18th, the bridge gave the engine room one and a half hours notice of arrival at Freetown, Sierra Leone, where they would take on fuel and water.

Two pilots boarded the ship. Although their presence was compulsory and they wore masses of gold braid on their white uniforms (plus a pair of thick heeled, bright green shoes on the feet of one of them) Captain Jackson took the ship alongside the quay himself, as he was informed by the pilots that masters usually bethed their own ships in that port!

The liner took on 1,867 tonnes of oil, completing the operation three hours earlier than had been expected, and sailed at 11 pm. Meanwhile, First Officer Phil Rentell, along with many others, busied himself in 'that old tropical tradition of watching a film on deck'! The pilots were dropped off as soon as possible as the *QE2* headed for Ascension Island.

The Equator had also been crossed and the troops had rigged an improvised swimming pool for the 'Crossing the Line' ceremony which had been extended to anyone in the vicinity of the pool, a foul smelling concoction being liberally dispensed.

The 19th brought with it the Doldrums with flat calms suddenly lashed by torrential rains and fierce, sudden squalls. Orders were received that the liner should keep 50 miles away from Ascension and that helicopters would ferry stores and personnel between the island and the ship.

Thursday 20th May marked the Christian festival of Ascension Day. On this day, in 1501, Ascension Island was discovered by the Portuguese João de Nova and now, in 1982, the *QE2* appropriately arrived at her position fifty miles to the west of the island in the early afternoon. But before she arrived another ship was sighted. Captain Jackson turned the *QE2* towards it only to find it was another Russian AIG, the *Primorye*. If he had been informed of its presence the captain felt that he could have avoided the unwanted meeting. An RAF Nimrod also reported an Argentinian ship, the *Chubut*, in the vicinity.

By three o'clock *HMS Dumbarton Castle*, normally a fishery/oil rig protection vessel, was stationed off the liner's starboard side and two helicopters transferred stores from the naval ship to the giant Cunarder.

This completed, the liner steamed to and fro off the island during the night (with an improvised black-out in force) waiting for the arrival of Major General Jeremy Moore and two hundred of his General Staff, who were flying out from the UK that night, plus additional troops and stores all of which would be shipped the next day.

Strict black-out would be imposed south of Ascension and templates for different sized windows and portholes had meanwhile been made, black plastic sheeting being cut to the various shapes. These were then taped to the hundreds of windows and portholes and Phil Rentell, acting under the instructions of Captain James of Royal Navy Party 1980, checked the results of his supervision by flying around the ship at night in a helicopter. The ship, as Captain James said, had been turned from 'the brightest star on the ocean, to the darkest'.

One unfortunate side effect of the black-out arrangements was to raise the internal temperature of the liner quite considerably, the black-out creating a greenhouse effect with the plastic wrinkling from the increased temperature.

Captain Jackson went onto the bridge at 11 pm and noted '. . . a frightening sight, to see this ship belting along at 27 knots on a black night and without a light showing'.

A rendezvous had been arranged by the higher command for Cunard's *Atlantic Causeway* to transfer various stores to the *QE2* on the 22nd. Unfortunately nobody had told the *Causeway* of the intended rendezvous and the ship initially (1 am) refused to identify herself. Eventually the container vessel asked the troopship, 'for what reason do we have the pleasure of this visit?'

The two ships steamed in company, still in the vicinity of Ascension Island, and helicopter transfer of stores started at 7 am, finishing about three hours later.

The *Queen* soon left the *Atlantic Causeway* (the sister ship to the *Atlantic Conveyor* that would be sunk three days later by the Argentinians) and Ascension far behind as she increased speed on completion of her tasks and she soon left Ascension far behind.

That night black-out was rigorously enforced, navigation lights and radars were switched off, and the ship became electronically silent: the latter precaution to deny a homing signal to enemy missiles. Navigation would now rely on the 'Mark 1 eyeball'!

As the *Queen* headed south it was initially thought that she would effect a rendezvous with the *Nordic* and *Baltic* ferries between South Georgia and the Falklands.

Alex Hutcheson took the Church Service on Sunday 23rd as the captain had, like many others on board, gone down with the 'flu' and had retired early.

Exercising of all kinds still continued with special attention being given to life saving and its associated appliances.

The regimental evenings that had been held ceased as the *Queen* approached the war zone. These unit dinners had been great fun with speeches and presentations, but the regimental bands playing within the confines of the Theatre Bar or the Q4 Bar provided a sound that had to be heard to be believed!

By the 25th the *QE2* had sailed far enough south of the Equator to meet the approaching winter chill of the Southern Hemisphere. Once again the officers changed uniform, returning to wearing their warmer 'blues'.

Browning automatic guns were placed on the mounting platforms that had been constructed on each bridge wing during the voyage down and Blowpipe missiles were fitted around the funnel. The *Queen* was now in a very small way, prepared for what she might meet.

The ship was, by now heading towards a rendezvous with the battle scarred County Class destroyer *HMS Antrim* in a position ninety miles north of South Georgia.

During the night of 26-27th May the radar was switched on, briefly, every thirty minutes and at 11 pm two stationary 'targets' were seen on the screen, five miles to port. Icebergs!

Captain Jackson was called at half past two in the morning. It was flat calm and many targets were seen on the radar screen (the captain later wrote: 'No way could it be a fishing fleet!') and the ship was put on Ice Routine. At one time more than a hundred bergs could be seen in the illuminated sweep of the radar arm and the captain ordered a reduction in speed as the *QE2* weaved around the ice: '. . . don't want to be the *Titanic* of the South Atlantic' he wrote, '. . . never have I known such a harrowing experience'.

The reduction in speed meant a late meeting with *HMS Antrim* but the delay had been justified. Morning light showed thick fog, becoming patchy, and a radar check at 11 am indicated *Antrim* to be nineteen miles away.

Three quarters of an hour later the two ships had stopped within one mile of each other, and the transfer of Major General Moore, Brigadier Wilson and their staffs commenced.

On the first full day at sea *QE2* rendezvoused with RFA *Grey Rover* to rehearse 'Replenishment at Sea'. A token ton of oil was taken on board from the oiler to prove that the operation could be successfully accomplished. *Captain Peter Jackson*

Whilst sailing off Ascension the *QE2* received Major General Jeremy Moore who arrived from the island by Chinook helicopter. *Captain Peter Jackson*

Arriving at South Georgia the *QE2* began to 'cross deck' her cargo of troops by requisitioned trawlers and 'VERT-REP' stores by helicopter.
Imperial War Museum

The sea was undulating in a long swell and although the senior officers, 'cross-decked' by helicopter, other troops had to transfer by ship's boats.

The swell caused a great strain on the bed plates of the Cunarder's davits and at least one was damaged. The troops had to jump to get on to the *Antrim* and in doing so one soldier broke a leg.

The transfer operations were over by 1.40 pm and the *QE2* sailed on, still amidst patchy fog and ice. The temperature at noon had been 3°C. Hundreds of icebergs had been visible since the rising sun had bathed them in changing colours of red and gold, until their 'tablecloths' of fog had cascaded over their sides to eventually obscure them. The numbers of icebergs had decreased as *Antrim* was closed but steadily increased once again as the *QE2* left the rendezvous position. One particular berg was reported as being three hundred feet high and a mile long!

Black darkness fell at 5 pm and, just after 6 pm, South Georgia was visible on the radar. The Right Whale Rocks were discerned and half an hour later two shackles of starboard anchor cable were let out. These hung, suspended from the hawse pipe into the deep water, in readiness for the final anchoring. If all the required shackles were paid out at once the force would have torn the cable clench out of the chain locker structure and the anchor lost.

The anchor was finally let go just after seven in the evening as the liner entered Cumberland Bay. Philip Rentell was in charge of the mooring party and from his position on the prow of the ship could not see the bridge in the prevailing murk, even though lights were now on. Ten shackles of cable were let out in a shower of sparks and rust. Only two were left in the locker by the time the cable brake took its hold, bringing to a halt the heart-stopping rattle that exuded from the liner's hawse pipes.

Canberra had been waiting impatiently for the *QE2* for several hours in the confines of the bay. The rust-streaked P&O liner had seen much action in Falkland Sound and her crew were becoming veterans of the sudden air attack. The liner had on board survivors from the sunken *HMS Ardent* and would transfer these to the *QE2*. The latter ship would in turn transfer, by boat and helicopter, her cargo of troops and stores.

The requisitioned trawler *Cordella* came alongside at 9.20 pm and left for the *Canberra* with the first batch of troops just after 11 pm.

Just before midnight *HMS Leeds Castle*, the *Cordella* and the Admiralty tug *Typhoon* came alongside to take off the last troops for the night, operations ceasing until morning as the combined perils of darkness and black-out made safe navigation and working imprudent.

From one captain to another.   *Courtesy of Captain Peter Jackson*

To Captain Peter Jackson with many thanks from all in Endurance   Nick Barker.

From six o'clock on the morning of Friday 28th May baggage, stores and troops were once more transferred to the waiting ships, either by sea or by air. The sea transport consisted of the *QE2's* lifeboats, the trawlers *Cordella, Junella, Northella, Farnella* and *Pict* (collectively known in naval parlance – along with other requisitioned ships including the *QE2* – as *STUFT,* or Ships Taken Up From Trade). The air transport was by many lifts by the helicopters, their operation being called 'Vertical Replenishment', or VERT-REP.

As well as the *Canberra*, the North Sea ferry *Norland* was also waiting for troops. *HMS Endurance*, the British Ice Patrol ship, was also in Cumberland Bay, maintaining a naval presence.

Canberra sailed at 10.30 pm after taking on hundreds of soldiers and the *QE2's* Sea King helicopters, in turn transferring the survivors of *HMS Ardent* to the care available on the *QE2. Norland* had similarly brought men from the sunken frigate *Antelope*. Work continued throughout the night and at four in the morning snow began to fall, covering the *QE2* in a thin white sheet. This, and the presence of patchy but dense fog caused the captain to remark 'what a climate!'.

Saturday, a Cunard cargo ship, the *Saxonia*, arrived for cargo and the Royal Fleet auxiliary *Stromness* brought yet more survivors, this time from the Type 42 destroyer *HMS Coventry*. The *Stromness* would afterwards take on the ammunition for which *Canberra* did not have time to wait.

The *QE2* had not remained immune from damage during her stay in South Georgia, but fortunately this had not been suffered as a result of the conflict. The platform lifts that descended from the boat deck to the sea were damaged by trawlers coming too heavily alongside and more davit bed plates were cracked during boat retrieval operations. The day before a badly corroded pipe in Seven Deck swimming pool had burst causing a widespread flood, damaging the Sauna, darkroom, working alleyway, crew quarters and the laundry.

During the day icebergs drifted into the entrance of Cumberland Bay and then, as if realising that their presence created an anathema, drifted out again onto the wanton highway of the wintry South Atlantic.

A group of crew members were taken ashore for a look around the derelict whaling station of Grytviken. Captain Jackson

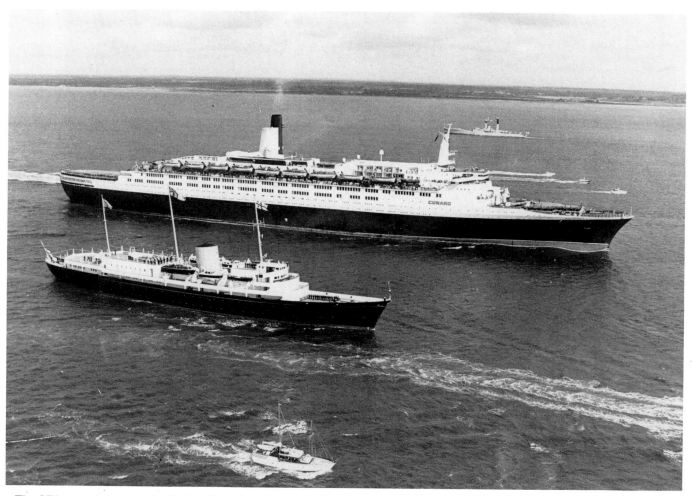

The *QE2* steamed slowly up the English Channel to ensure that her meeting with the Royal Yacht *Britannia*, carrying Her Majesty, The Queen Mother, happened on time. With survivors from *HMS Coventry* on the forward heli-pad, *HMS's Ardent* and *Antelope's* survivors aft and the *QE2's* own company on the Boat Deck the liner exchanged greetings with the Royal Yacht.

Courtesy of Captain Peter Jackson

was to have gone ashore with them but changed his mind: on his late visit to the bridge on the previous evening he had noticed that the barometer had started to fall so he was now anxious to get the last of the troops off his ship before the promised deterioration in the weather set in, an harbinger of the fast approaching winter.

By four o'clock in the afternoon a north westerly gale was making conditions hazardous: the last sixty men disembarked into the trawlers which were having problems in mooring safely without breaking their ropes. *Junella* was to be the last ship alongside, taking off stores and as soon as she left, at 5.30 pm, the *QE2* started to weigh anchor.

Passing by Banff Point fifteen minutes later the liner increased speed to 18 knots.

Two hours later *QE2* was again in the icefield but, with judicious navigation, she emerged safely at 10 pm;

Lifeboat practice was held on Sunday but the warship survivors were initially unhappy about congregating in the liner's aluminium superstructure, but their fears were allayed by the supervising officers.

Monday was a very uncomfortable day at sea and only the forward set of stabilisers was used. Two drums of hydrochloric acid broke loose in Two Deck baggage room and the chief officer was sent to get them under control.

Just under nine hundred tons of fuel oil were left in the tanks by Tuesday, enough only for a day and a half's steaming.

To replenish the ship, arrangements were made to rendezvous with the *RFA Bayleaf* and the two ships met in the late afternoon.

The sea was too rough to allow the operation to commence and as it would soon be dark the *Bayleaf* took up an overnight station astern of the *QE2*.

The RFA drifted away from the *Queen* during the night and it was not until nine the next morning that a line was transferred between ships and the refuelling commenced. When the oiling had been completed by 6.30 nearly four thousand tons of top grade admiralty oil had been given to the *QE2*. The operation (carried out in a westerly Force 7 with an accompanying rough sea – although the sky was bright but cloudy) had finished just in time as the chaffing caused by the two ships' movements had caused the connections on the *Queen* to be worn to a point of danger.

In the early evening the captain received a message to say that the *QE2* was to proceed to Southampton and at 7 pm Captain James R.N. told the crew. Many were disappointed as they had anticipated that the *Queen* would put the survivors ashore at Ascension and then return to the war zone. The news was not released in Britain until 6th June, by which time the liner had left the danger zone after stopping off at Ascension.

After their various ordeals the survivors from HM Ships *Ardent*, *Antelope* and *Coventry* relaxed in the free days at sea taking benefit, as many other people do, from the refreshing regime of a sea cruise. Gradually their spirits picked up and eventually they organised a bawdy 'Sod's Opera' which they performed in the Double Down Room to popular acclaim.

Ascension was reached on 4th June, and *HMS Dumbarton Castle* once again met the liner. The *QE2* was once more on her way by 6 pm after a three hour stay during which time the *Dumbarton Castle* had taken off personnel including six SAS men who had survived a helicopter crash on the South American mainland. A public landing in Southampton would have been against the interests of their security.

By now it was known that the Queen Mother wished to greet the *QE2* as the liner returned to the United Kingdom on Friday 11th June.

The naval survivors possessed only the clothes that they were rescued in or had been given by the liner's company. So flying stations were sounded and a helicopter flew off the ship as she steamed near Mount's Bay, Cornwall, on 10th June.

New uniforms were brought out to the ship (plus a liberal supply of fresh Cornish pasties!) and both naval and civilian personnel readied themselves for their royal reception.

Several visitors were flown out to the ship on the bright Friday morning of the *QE2*'s homecoming.

At seven in the morning forty newsmen arrived on the ship followed at eight by Admiral Sir John Fieldhouse and Lord Matthews and half-an-hour later by Ralph Bahna. The pilot, Captain Driver, came aboard at 8.48 am.

A message was received from the Royal Yacht *Britannia* from which H.M. The Queen Mother would welcome the ship:
'Captain P. Jackson.

I am pleased to welcome you back as *Queen Elizabeth 2* returns to home waters, after your tour of duty in the South Atlantic. The exploits of your own ship's company and the deeds of valour of those who served in *Antelope, Coventry* and *Ardent*

have been acclaimed throughout the land, and I am proud to add my personal tribute.

Elizabeth Regina, Queen Mother.'
Captain Jackson replied immediately:
'Please convey to Her Majesty Queen Elizabeth, the Queen Mother, our thanks for her kind message. Cunard's *Queen Elizabeth 2* is proud to have been of service to Her Majesty's Forces.

Jackson. Master QE2.'

The *QE2* passed the famous Needles lighthouse on the western tip of the Isle of Wight at 9 am. Fifteen minutes later, after passing between Yarmouth and Hurst Castle, the *Royal Yacht Britannia* was abeam and, as the liner steamed by the Royal Yacht, the figure of the Queen Mother could be seen, dressed in pale blue, on its after deck. The *QE2*'s company and the warship survivors gave three cheers and the liner blew her siren in salute.

From the *QE2* to the Royal Yacht:
'Please convey to Her Majesty Queen Elizabeth with humble duty the Master, Officers and ratings of the Royal and Merchant Navies embarked in *QE2*, join in offering their loyal greetings.'

The *QE2* was almost home. Surrounded by small craft, buzzed by light aircraft and watched by thousands lining the Solent and other vantage points she progressed in state past Calshot, then by the tankers at Fawley which, once again, blew their own greetings. She slowly sailed up Southampton Water to the Queen Elizabeth II terminal in Southampton Docks.

From the quay a sea of faces watched the liner, many looking for loved ones, and banners held high bore messages of greeting. The *QE2* was turned in mid-stream by her tugs and at mid-day came to rest, port side along the jetty.

After steaming 14,967 miles and consuming 10,287 tonnes of fuel, the *Queen* was home!

Elizabeth R

Luncheon
on the occasion of the visit of
Her Majesty Queen Elizabeth,
The Queen Mother,
on board Queen Elizabeth 2
to unveil the South Atlantic Plaque,
2nd December 1982

Host: The Lord Matthews

Wines

Batard Montrachet 1980
(Moillard)

Chateau Gruaud Larose 1966
Second Growth St Julien

Luncheon

Coquille of Fresh Lobster

Roast Saddle of Southdown Lamb

Fresh Broccoli Spears,
Parisienne Potatoes

Fresh Pear, Liqueur Sauce

Petits Fours

Selection of
English Cheeses with Celery

Coffee

Her Majesty Queen Elizabeth the Queen Mother signed Captain Jackson's menu after a very special luncheon held on board. *Courtesy of Captain Peter Jackson*

Chapter Eleven

The Brightest Star on the Ocean

Following her trooping duties in the South Atlantic the *Queen Elizabeth 2* had to be refurbished, reconverting and renovating her once again to 'the brightest star on the ocean'.

Before disembarking at South Georgia the troops had cleaned the ship as best they could, removing marks where boots had scuffed the bulkheads and so on. But the helipads had to be removed at Southampton, and Cunard took the opportunity to re-style some of the rooms.

The work of converting the liner to a troopship had taken a mere eight days but this would now take nine weeks to put right. QE2 spent much of the time in the King George V dry dock in Southampton prior to being berthed alongside a quay in the New Dock, receiving the final touches there.

She emerged from the refit ready for her first post Falklands sailing on 14th August with a pleasant alteration to her appearance. Her funnel casing that had previously been painted white now reappeared in the traditional Cunard colours of red with two, eight inch black stripes, the inner tubular casing providing the black top. Each of these bands was made up of two widths of four inch tape, soon to be flapping in the Atlantic breeze.

But the immediate impact to the eye was in the colouring of the hull. The dark, almost black, charcoal grey had been over painted with a light 'pebble' grey. Apparently so painted on the instructions of Lord Matthews, chairman of Cunard. The paint scheme proved to be unpractical as well as unpopular, soon displaying scuff marks from the nudging bows of New York tugs and unsightly streaks of rust that dribbled down the vessel's sides from portholes and anchor hawse pipes.

The liner thankfully reverted to her original hull colour of charcoal grey a few months later. To the ship-lover she then almost wore the traditional colours of the old Cunard ships and more than ever deserved, through livery and action, the title of *Queen*.

Internally, changes had been effected to maintain the QE2's position as leader amongst cruise ships. The Six Deck swimming pool became part of a prestigious 'Golden Door' fitness complex, expensive to use on shore but freely available to the ship's passengers. The exclusive Queen's Grill was enlarged, as was the Casino, and a start was made on the creation of a Club Lido on the aft area of Quarter Deck. This lido would be completed in Germany during an extensive refit in late 1983 when a Magrodome, a retractable glazed sun-roof devised by MaeGregor-Navire (a company familiar with special hatch covers), was fitted over the first class swimming pool making the area habitable during even the early and late Atlantic seasons.

Many bands, large and small, professional and amateur, often entertain the *QE2's* passengers from the quayside. The Highbury Area Band from Portsmouth play the *Queen* away shortly after her return from the Falklands.
Steve Dymock

It was during this particular refit that the aft verandah windows were substantially altered and new, large capacity enclosed luxury motor boats, carried on heavy davits, were fitted at the aft end of the boat deck.

The QE2's built-in ability to accept change has been proven on several occasions, the design of her internal spaces lending themselves to alterations in function or arrangement.

Amongst the many changes that have been effected over the years the early alterations were the ones that would cause most comment as, during the course of the work, some of the orignal rooms disappeared making way for new.

The London Gallery, once used as a display area for British art, eventually became the Computer Learning Centre. Once American restrictions on casinos had been lifted the spaces occupied by the Upper Deck Library and the Port Foyer found themselves amalgamated into one in 1972 to cater for the new demand. The Lookout Bar, the only public room to have had a forward looking view, was unfortunately sacrificed to become a kitchen for the new blue and white Queen's Grill, (latterly a casino but formerly the 736 Club which had been described as 'noteworthy' by the shipping press), that would cater for the occupants of the newly fitted luxury penthouses.

These penthouses were fitted in three stages and in three countries, over a period of fifteen years. The preparation for the fitting of the first of these luxury rooms took place whilst the liner was still at sea in early 1972 in readiness for when the QE2 would be taken out of service in October for her first major refit.

The prefabricated aluminium blocks of luxury cabins (which included the Queen Anne and Trafalgar suites in which the occupants had the distinction of being able to go upstairs to bed) were fitted in two halves, port and starboard. During the same refit other luxury cabins were built on Boat Deck sites previously occupied by shops and store rooms, and the old Grill Room became part of an enlarged Columbia Restaurant. The Britannia Restaurant underwent a change of name and re-appeared as Tables of the World. In 1987 the restaurant underwent another change becoming the Mauretania Restaurant.

The second smaller block of rooms, sited immediately aft of the mast, was fitted in Bayonne, New Jersey, in 1977, resulting in the Queen Mary and Queen Elizabeth Suites. The third block, aft of the first and forward of the funnel, was fitted in the most recent reconstruction in Germany in 1987.

The £2 million refit of 1972 also saw other major changes carried out, the principle work being the reconstruction of the Main Kitchen to one of a highly sophisticated American design. Minor bulkheads were erected, new tiled floors laid, stainless steel fittings and old ovens were replaced and new windows cut during the course of the work. The addition of the new windows spotlighted a serious problem in the reconstruction work. The daylight that now filled the new kitchen shone through a fine, powdery mist. Much to the horror of the workforce, this was found to emanate from the American insulating sheeting being used which, unbeknown to the men using it, was asbestos based, the necessary precautions not having been taken - until then!

Because of the difficulties in fitting out the American kitchen, the seven week refit took rather longer than had been anticipated, the liner finally leaving Southampton two and a half days late. To Cunard's annoyance Vosper Thornycroft had not given notice of the delay until ten hours before the original time of sailing. However, the ruffled relationship between the two companies was soon smoothed and Cunard admitted to being delighted with the work.

Because of all the work carried out on the passenger areas the gross tonnage of the liner has risen over the years. When the ship was still being built it was expected that she would be 58,000 gross tons but, after the restructuring of classes during building, she appeared at 65,862 tons.

The liner, after many modifications, is now 67,139 gross tons and although larger purpose built, light draught cruise ships have been, or are planned to be, constructed, she is still one of the largest true transatlantic liners ever to have been built.

The run-up to the notable changes that were effected to the Queen Elizabeth 2 in 1972 had their beginnings in the latter half of 1971 when a great change happened to Cunard itself. In spite of a poor financial year in 1970 Cunard was doing well but, due to various factors, the company found itself at the centre of a takeover bid.

The successful bidder from several contenders, buying the company for £26 million, was Trafalgar House. Already owners of civil engineering concerns, hotels and industrial activities (amongst many others) the company would add Cunard to its list of hotel interests.

Victor Matthews became the new chairman of Cunard and Sir Basil Smallpeice transferred to the board of Trafalgar House. He remained there for five months after the last board meeting of Cunard was held as an independant company, on 25th August 1971.

Sir Basil found that, after rescuing Cunard from near collapse, he could no longer effectively assist the company in his new position and 'let myself quietly over the side and went ashore. . . . . with sadness in my heart. . . .'

Since the early years QE2 has enjoyed Royal patronage and in September 1988 will be the venue of a special lunch which will be attended by H.M. The Queen Mother. This will be to mark the 50th anniversary of the launch of H.M.'s illustrious namesake, the first Queen Elizabeth, on 27th September 1938 and amongst the honoured guests, both at the lunch and subsequent commemorative voyage, will be the liner's last captain, Geoffrey Marr.

The Queen Mother was previously on board in May 1986, meeting retired Cunard employees and passengers who had sailed on the Queen Mary's maiden voyage fifty years earlier. The liner had then sailed on a voyage to commemorate the debut of that remarkable ship, Britain's best loved liner, carrying along with the veterans from that premier trip the Mary's last skipper, Captain John Treasure Jones.

After the QE2's return from the Falklands the Queen Mother expressed a wish to visit the liner that she had greeted on its return from active service. This she did in December 1982 and took the opportunity to unveil a plaque on which was engraved the message that she had sent to Captain Jackson welcoming him, the ship and the ship's company and passengers back to the United Kingdom.

Three weeks after the liner's reintroduction into service after the Falklands episode the QE2 broke down off Falmouth. It was one more in a series of engine breakdowns that were becoming both increasingly expensive and worrying to Cunard.

One of the more dramatic breakdowns had occurred in 1974 whilst the QE2 was on a south-bound cruise from New York. The causes reflected an incident that had called a halt to her technical trials from Greenock in 1968.

The liner had left New York for a cruise to Bermuda on the evening of Saturday 30th March 1974 with 1, 648 passengers on board, including almost 800 senior citizens, and 1,041 crew.

As soon as she was out into the open waters of the Atlantic she ran into rough weather, rough enough to prevent the pilot from being landed. Speed had to be maintained; to decrease it would have nullified the effect of the ship's stabilisers.

Conditions were very much the same on the following day and the captain, Peter Jackson, cancelled the obligatory life-boat

With the twin towers of the World Trade Center dominating a receding Manhattan skyline the *QE2* heads for the open sea. *Cunard*

drill, the prevailing conditions making it dangerous for the passengers, especially the elderly, to try to reach the Boat Deck.

Captain Jackson also made a broadcast (his maxim was 'always keep passengers informed', and to tell them: 'If you hear rumours, ask whether the perpetrator had got it from the captain!') and advised the passengers to stay in their cabins. To this end he took the unusual step of cancelling the Sunday divine service due to be held in the Theatre.

During the evening, as the liner travelled further south, the weather moderated. It was hoped to hold the cancelled boat drill the next day.

These plans were rudely shattered when, at four o'clock the next morning (1st April), the ship came to a standstill in the water.

The captain was told that, because two pipes (one oil, one boiler feed water) had been wrongly connected, oil had contaminated the boiler feed water - water which has to be extremely pure, four parts in a million.

Fortunately by now the weather had calmed and the engineers set to in cleaning the system, working hard all day. The captain made many telephone calls to Cunard and once again cancelled the delayed boat drill considering that, under the current circumstances, it would have an unnecessarily negative psychological effect on the passengers - especially the elderly.

The liner continued to drift and the telephoned remedial action suggested by Cunard's technical department in London was effective for only half an hour.

By Tuesday morning the liner had reached a position of 29° 26'N, 68°06', approximately 275 miles south west of Bermuda.

Oil was still contaminating the port boiler and there was at least another ten hours of cleaning to do. Because of the situation much of the liner's hotel services had been shut down; the air-conditioning was shut off; the lifts were not operating (these were essential for the old folk); refrigeration had been switched off, the kitchens ceased to fully function and lighting was kept to a bare minimum. But it was the cessation of the operation of

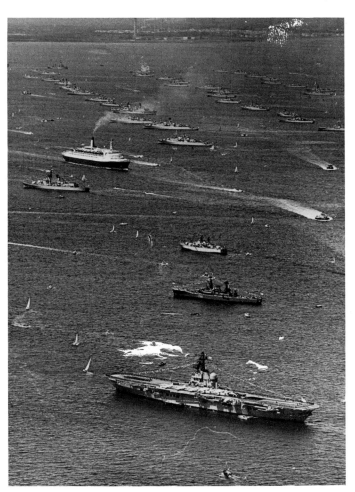

Threading her way through the 1977 NATO Fleet Review the *QE2* provided an elegant splash of colour amongst the various shades of grey of the parading warships. *Southern Newspapers*

59

the desalination plant that supplied the ship's hotel services' fresh water (there was only five days supply left much of which would be used to flush through the contaminated machinery) that caused the greatest concern.

The captain knew that the nearest available large tug was 600 miles away so he put a suggestion to Cunard.

As a result of the captain's recommendations, which were approved by Cunard, the Norwegian cruise liner *Sea Venture* was sent to assist the *Queen*.

For this to happen special dispensations had to be sought from both British and Norwegian authorities. The *Sea Venture* was licensed to carry 600, only a fraction of the *QE2's* complement, but arrangements were made to cover any discrepancies both in legal and amenity aspects. In the end, the *Venture* was sanctioned to carry an extra 1,000 passengers.

The white Norwegian knight in the form of the *Sea Venture* arrived on the scene at three in the morning of 3rd April, ready to assist the distressed *Queen*.

The one way transfer between ships (almost anticipating the movements occurring during the Falklands campaign) started at 4 am with life jackets and twenty life-rafts from the *QE2* going over to the Norwegian ship to bring the *Venture's* life-saving capability up to legal requirements.

Essential stores followed and, at 7.30 am, the first passengers descended the forward and aft starboard accommodation ladders to board the waiting launches that had been lowered from both liners.

By 3.50 in the afternoon the last of the passengers had disembarked from the *QE2* and an hour later the liner had recovered her boats. The *Sea Venture's* launches continued to transfer stores and baggage until 5.40 am when she hoisted her boats from the sea, sailing for Bermuda ten minutes later.

A total of 1,654 people had been transferred during one of the most unusual operations ever carried out at sea. This number, incidentally, included six crew members who would help with the disembarkation at Bermuda.

The next day two tugs, *Elizabeth Moran* and *Joan Moran*, arrived at 2.13 pm and, seventy five minutes later, started the tow.

As the *Queen* and her entourage approached Bermuda the pilot boarded and two more tugs, *Bermudian* and *Faithful*, came to assist in the liners' passage through the Narrows to Murray's Anchorage.

Here the boilers were purged and the *QE2* was able to sail for New York at 16 knots using two boilers.

After further work at Todd's shipyard the *QE2* sailed for Southampton, still only on two boilers but achieving 24 knots. The voyage home took six days instead of the usual five.

On the liner's initial technical trials from Greenock in 1968 her engines had performed well; her pilot described her as 'handling like a motor car'.

But from the breakdown of the turbines during the ensuing full-scale trials to the Canaries to the breakdown off Falmouth, Cornwall, just after her return to service after the Falklands the engines and boilers have proved expensive to maintain. Many spare parts have had to be specially made by hand and this costly maintenance, along with the astronomic increases in oil fuel prices since the ship was built and high manning costs, caused the Cunard Line to appraise the future of the *QE2*.

They came to a momentous decision.

The *Queen*, if she was to be economically viable and if she was to continue to sail for another twenty years, would have to be re-engined.

Although extremely expensive this would be far cheaper than building a new, similar vessel.

After the initial decision was made a meeting was held in Southampton in mid 1983 to which various contenders from ship-building and engineering firms were invited. Each firm then submitted ideas and tenders for the forthcoming mammoth conversion with Cunard placing the contract with their final choice - the German shipyard of Lloyd Werft in Bremerhaven.

This yard had converted the giant ex-French transatlantic liner *France* into the Norwegian cruiseship *Norway* during the winter of 1979; the yard had also done previous work on the *QE2* including the fitting of the retractable Magrodome and the fitting of a new bulbous bow.

Cunard had for several years favoured foreign yards for the refits of their flagships. British yards had for a long time been shedding expensive manpower and were therefore able in recent years to perform only the lesser tasks in ship repair and maintenance. Unions and public bodies took this export work as a snub to Britain but Cunard had, in between, spent £millions in the U.K. in keeping the liner at sea.

British firms would, on this occasion too, be awarded many of the major sub-contracts that would emanate from the forthcoming conversion. Foremost amongst these would be firms belonging to the giant General Electric Company (GEC). It was part of this company, that under its original title of Associated Electrical Industries (AEI) that had built much of the *QE2's* original electrical machinery, such as the three turbine generators then the largest afloat.

It now fell to AEI's successor, GEC Large Machines Limited of Rugby, to build the two 350 ton, 44 megawatt electric propulsion motors, as the liner was to be converted from steam to diesel-electric propulsion. GEC Turbine Generators Limited, Stafford, would build nine electric generators and the company's Industrial Controls division, also at Rugby, would provide the synchro convertors that would start the motors and provide the slow speed operation of the ship. The engine control room console would be supplied by GEC Electrical Projects who would also co-ordinate all the company's efforts.

The turbine generators would be fitted alongside their power source, nine MAN-B&W diesels, which would be fitted five in the after engine room and four in the forward. The work of installing diesels, associated machinery, fuel treatment plant, generators and motors, would be likened to open heart surgery.

The contract to convert the *QE2* was signed on 24th October 1985 which gave Lloyd Werft almost a year in which to organise their own subcontractors - there were fifty major ones - and to advance their own preparations for the conversion.

QE2 arrived in Southampton for the last time as a steamship on October 25th before leaving for Bremerhaven. Cunard's magnificent flagship arrived at the German shipyard on 27th October 1986 and the carefully planned work began immediately.

The first major job was to strip out the boilers, turbines and other redundant machinery. This was done by removing the funnel and using the emptied shaft below as a passageway - both for removing scrap material and installing the new machinery.

Great care was taken in the removal of the old equipment and, because of the presence of asbestos in the insulation, a delay in the work was caused. This was undesirable as Lloyd Werft were liable to pay penalties for any delays by the day.

Eckart Knoth, chairman of Lloyd Werft, described the stripping-out process as being 'like hell'. By the time it was complete 4,700 tons of scrapped turbines, boilers, pipes and other broken organs of the *Queen* lay on the quayside, dominated by the comparatively still pristine - but to be modified - funnel.

The emptied machinery spaces appeared cavernous with heavy-lift trucks being dwarfed by the surroundings in which they now incongruously moved.

When the liner was being built in Scotland, twenty years previously, a scale model of the engine room had been made to show the location of each and every piece of equipment and pipe.

Looking very forlorn the *Queen* sits in the Kaiserdock II dry dock, Bremerhaven, whilst her engine room, interior, propellers and new penthouse suites are gutted, refurbished and fitted. The P & O liner *Canberra* came in during the *QE2's* stay for a refit, although less extensive, of her own.
Lloyd Werft, Bremerhaven

Similarly, now, a model was made of the new layout and many problems were ironed out well beforehand.

The first major items of machinery to be installed were the British-made electric propulsion motors, shipped to Germany in sections and reassembled at the shipyard, which were carefully lowered through the temporary hatchway and slid aft.

A large floating crane, HEBE 2, performed all the heavy lifting tasks, her lifting capacity of 750 tons being more than adequate for the weights of the *QE2's* machinery.

Then came the nine, four-stroke, nine cylinder diesel engines which were also lowered and slid into place on their seatings in the ultimately unmanned engine rooms.

One of the mini MAN-B&W 9L 58/64 diesel engines on its test bed in Augsburg. *MAN-B&W*

A complete electrical generator shown prior to its packing and shipment to Germany. *GEC Turbine Generators Limited*

Top: Reappearing slightly 'thickened about the waist' after her major 1987 refit, the *QE2* is ready for her third decade in service.

Cedric Wasser

Left: The Queen's Room as it now appears. The original chairs which reflected the trumpet-like columns have been replaced by cubic armchairs in soft brown leather. Perhaps less pleasing to the eye than the former, they are much easier in which to remain seated! *Cunard*

Below left: The refurbished swimming pool on One Deck Lido now boasts a vivid Cunard lion in mosaic tiles. *Cunard*

Below right: The spectacular Columbia Restaurant with its 750 seat capacity. *Cunard*

Top: The Double Up Room was one of the public rooms to be dramatically altered in the 1987 refit. Now called the Grand Lounge, the old stainless steel stairway has gone (the new one is sited at the opposite end of the room) and shops have encroached even further into the upper (Double Up) lounge area. *Cunard*

Centre left: A white piano with a glass top and surrounding glass bar provided the focal point in the new (1987) Yacht Club bar (ex Double Down Bar) on the Upper Deck. *Cunard*

Centre right: This view illustrates the plush conditions in the cabins awaiting the first class passenger. *Cunard*

Right: The corridor of the new suites fitted in Bremerhaven by Lloyd Werft. This view will be seen only by those few privileged to travel in this exclusive accommodation. *Cunard*

The nine engines, MAN-B&W L58/64 (ie, the cylinders were 580 millimetres in diameter and the pistons moved through a 640 millimetre stroke) were named Alpha, Bravo, Charlie etc. up to number 9 which was India.

Part of the contract stipulated that the liner should achieve 28.5 knots on 85% of the engine power and that there should be no increase in vibration over that induced by the now displaced machinery.

To overcome any vibration problem the engines were mounted on layered rubber resilient mounts, placed at an angle to the engine seats, which would keep vibration to an absolute minimum.

With her old, smooth-running steam turbines the *QE2*, at 28.5 knots, had used six hundred tons of oil fuel a day, thus burning up 120,000 tons per year (at £100 per ton). With her new engines consumption would hopefully be reduced to 270 tons a day.

The waste heat from the machinery would also be put to good use. It would be utilised to heat accommodation, to pre-heat the thick oil fuel, provide steam to the various hotel services and help to produce one thousand tons of fresh water a day from the sea via four Serck vacuum evaporators. Another 450 tons per day would be produced from the sea by Reverse Osmosis Plant equipment that had also provided additional fresh water on the Falklands 'cruise'.

The ability to produce more than enough fresh water would enable the liner to reduce her fresh water tankage by 40%.

At the 'business end' of all the propulsion machinery were the two propellers which had to absorb the enormous power produced by the nine diesels.

The *QE2* has always remained the largest, most powerful twin screw vessel in the world. Stone Manganese Marine, the manufacturers of her original six (fixed) bladed, 5791 millimetre diameter propellers had insisted that 110000 shp was the maximum that two propellers could absorb.

Now 130,000 shp was required to be absorbed and the Dutch firm of LIPS, of Drunen, had designed propellers with five blades each. But these blades were controllable, they could

be turned remotely on their bosses. This meant that the special astern machinery that was required with fixed blade propellers could be dispensed with as, by turning the controlled blades sufficiently, the liner could be halted and then sent astern whilst the propellers still rotated in the same direction.

The propellers would also be operated at only two speeds - 144 revolutions per minute for speeds above 18 knots and 72 revolutions for those below. The controlled pitch of the blades would do the rest, enabling the liner to go from 34 knots ahead to 19 knots astern.

The propeller blades were also 'skewed' - scimitar shaped - to cut down the effects of cavitation and to reduce the propeller induced vibration on the hull.

The new 5,800 millimetre diameter propellers were to be augmented by recently developed (but long theorised) pseudo-propellers called Grim wheels (named after their professor inventor). At 6.7 metres diameter they were larger than the propellers, had seven slender uniquely shaped blades (or vanes) and freely rotated at about one third of the CPPs' speed.

Their purpose was to absorb the waste thrust lost from the propellers. This was absorbed by the turbine like inner part of the vane and converted into thrust by the vane tip which thus acted like a second propeller. A worthwhile increase in efficiency of almost 4% was expected by the use of these wheels.

The old 32 ton, manganese bronze propellers were sold off. One would be retained as a dockland exhibit in England but its partner was scheduled to become the basis of two and a half thousand sets of high quality golf clubs!

Whilst the *Queen Elizabeth 2* was having a new heart installed into her very depths the shipyard was also restyling much of her accommodation, both passenger and crew. A study of the deck plans contained within this book will indicate the changes that have been made in these areas between the liner's building and major conversion in 1987.

The manning of the liner would also change under Cunard's new plans. The all British crew were given the chance of either contracting their labour or else accept a 'golden handshake' and hand their jobs over to other, perhaps foreign,

Shipshape once again the engine room is ready for business!
Cunard

BOAT DECK

UPPER DECK

QUARTER DECK

The main passenger decks as they appeared after their 1987 re-arrangement. It is interesting to compare these layouts with those from the time when the 963 foot long liner was built (see inside back cover).

Cunard

contractors. In spite of union protests that the men would be selling British jobs of which they were only 'temporary custodians', the liner now boasts a multi-national crew in line with other major cruise liners.

Suffice it to say that the whole conversion cost Cunard in excess of £92million, a price that was much cheaper than building an equivalent new ship. Of the cost £2 million alone went to restyling the Tables of the World - originally the Britannia - restaurant. Renamed in honour of the *Mauretania* (Cunard's venerable, record breaking and most loved liner of 1907) the restaurant displays an oversize painting of that liner leaving the shipyard as well as beautifully framed photographs taken on board and of her building and a magnificent model of the old four funnelled liner stands in a glass case for all to admire.

After an absence of many years in an ocean liner restaurant dancing has been re-introduced with the provision of dance floor facilities in both Columbia (another early Cunard transatlantic paddlesteamer) and Mauretania restaurants.

With the expenditure of 1,700,000 man-hours the biggest merchantship conversion ever undertaken was almost complete.

Trials had to be run in the North Sea to test the unification of the whole. These lasted from April 8th until the 22nd. Fuel consumption was as hoped for as were the speeds attained. The maximum speed achieved of 33.8 knots left many, including Cunard (in spite of historical precedents), wondering whether the liner would now contend for the legendary Blue Ribband still held by the American liner *United Stated*.

Testing the new power plant had taken the ship, travelling at full speed, 3 minutes 38 seconds to come to a halt in just over a mile! A further twelve minutes and she was going astern at 19 knots!

Vibration, too, was measurably down in the public rooms although it remained at a similar level as before in the aft sections of the ship.

Work continued during the trials in the hotel areas of the ship in an attempt to finish the uncompleted tasks before the liner left the shipyard. In spite of the frantic efforts workmen would travel with the ship to New York in an attempt to clear the backlog of unfinished work that still needed to be completed in cabins and to plumbing and air conditioning.

The shipyard handed over the QE2 to her owners on 25th April during a ceremony held on board. Eckart Knoth (chairman), Dieter Haake (managing director) and Werner Luken (project manager for the QE2) represented Lloyd Werft whilst Cunard's Ralph Bahna (president and managing director), Alan Kennedy (chairman) and project manager, Mike Novak - not to mention Captain Lawrence Portet - could look on a difficult job well done. The project had not been without its heartaches and moments of apprehension but the company was glad to have its ship back in good order, retrieved from the mess, noise and disorder that degrades the loveliest of ships when in shipyard hands.

Sir Nigel Broackes, chairman of Trafalgar House, was also present at the ceremony amongst the five hundred distinguished guests. He had hosted a party on board the evening before.

Lloyd Werft presented the QE2 with a special gift - a large, embossed leather marinescape that had originally hung in the First Class Smoking Room of the four funnelled, German record breaker *Kaiser Wilhelm der Grosse* of 1897.

For their part Cunard presented a cheque to the shipyard's welfare fund. In appreciation of the business that the shipping line had brought to his city, the Mayor of Bremerhaven gave a mahogany boxed compass to a smiling Ralph Bahna.

At last the time came for the liner to leave the shipyard that had instilled her with an invigorated hope for the future. She carried with her on her trip across the North Sea many special guests - and also several hundred shipyard workers frantically trying to finish those jobs which were left uncompleted in order to get the ship away from the shipyard in time.

In mid-July 1987 the *QE2* enters the King George V dry dock in Southampton to have the remaining vanes cut off the Grim wheel bosses.
Roger Hardingham

Work continued overnight on the liner with holes being cut in the bottom to provide windows through which to study the propellers' solo performances. *Philip Rentell*

The *QE2's* re-entry into service as almost a new ship called for a special honour - a second maiden voyage.

To mark this occasion Cunard had arranged for hundreds of Southampton children to join the liner for a special day trip down Southampton Water to the waters of the Solent between Hampshire and the Isle of Wight.

Here, Diana, Princess of Wales, would join the ship by launch and travel with the children back to Southampton. Once again the liner was 'buzzed' by two Harrier jump jets and, on reaching port, that other masterpiece of British mid-century engineering, Concorde, flew overhead - saluting the *Queen* to whom she owed so much of her own custom.

Early that evening the *Queen Elizabeth 2* left Southampton for New York, sailing for her American terminal for the first time not as a steamship, but as a motorship.

But before her arrival at Southampton from Germany on April 28th an unforseen incident took place without the knowledge or notice of those on board.

The liner had performed well whilst transiting the North Sea. Her new powers of speed had so impressed some of the navigating officers that they thought that the liner would 'overshoot the Isle of Wight'!

No one suspected that anything was amiss until a diver, inspecting the underwater hull during a security probe before the Princess of Wales' visit, found that each Grim wheel had lost five consecutive vanes, leaving the two remaining blades on each wheel raised in a grim victory salute.

This necessitated a hurried overnight drydocking during a turnaround on July 9th in the King George V Dry Dock, the work being done by Thew Engineering (the successors to Vosper Thornycroft Shiprepairers). The remaining blades were cut off and sent back to Holland for investigation.

The *Queen* ran for a year with bare wheel bosses but she is due to be dry docked in July 1988 when she will be fitted with new propellers.

Teething troubles were also experienced with the electric propulsion motors and during an early, post-conversion cruise spare parts had to be flown out from England to Gibraltar. The motors are still being brought up to perfection with additional fittings being planned for the future.

Vociferous complaints from a few passengers were made during and after the second maiden voyage. These were caused by the unfinished state of some cabins, the plumbing, air conditioning in some public rooms and the inexperience of some of the hotel staff. Many of the problems were due to the essentially newness of the liner, problems that could be expected on any new ship that has to be 'run in' before perfection is achieved.

At the time of writing the *QE2*, one of the great ships of all time, is the only ship left offering scheduled North Atlantic ferry voyages. Truly the last of a long line of a huge international fleet of illustrious predecessors, those travelling on board her can look back over a century and a half of shipping and be aware that the *Queen* has maintained the expected high standards of North Atlantic traditions to the last: the last 'Superliner to America'.

Douglas Ward, author of the 'Berlitz Complete Handbook to Cruising' and editor of 'Cruise Digest Reports' summed up the contemporary impact of the *QE2*: '*QE2* is now the most perfectly integrated passenger ship afloat. She has no equal - for no other ship can cross the Atlantic like the *Queen* - or provide such facilities and style for cruising.

She is, quite simply, the world's finest ship and the last of the true express ocean liners.

Without doubt, the most magnificent ship in the world. And very, very British.'

The last chapter for the *Queen Elizabeth 2* has yet to be written. By the time that this is done the 'New Cunarder' will undoubtedly have travelled many more thousands of miles, bringing pleasure to untold numbers of passengers.

May the *QE2* enjoy, as Her Majesty Queen Elizabeth II said during her launching speech:

'A long life and good fortune'.

To mark the final days of the *QE2* as a steamship several ex-skippers met on board. Included in this picture are Captain 'Bil' Warwick (right), Mortimer Hehir, Peter Jackson and Bob Arnott (third, fourth and fifth from right).
Southern Newspapers

Acknowledgements

In this necessarily brief account of the career of the *QE2* I have tried to paint a broad picture, highlighting some events and briefly touching on others. I apologise if I have missed out any favourite story about the ship but space, of course, precluded the inclusion of everything!

The *Queen* has had an amazingly action-packed career and, for some of the major headline stories in her twenty one years of being, I have endeavoured to obtain first-hand accounts. For these I am particularly grateful to: Boyd Haining, ex-Shipyard Manager at John Brown's Shipbuilders, Captain Peter Jackson and First Officer Philip Rentell. Eric Flounders, Cunard's Public Relations Manager in London, has been equally helpful in his encouragement and support.

Cunard's shore staff of two continents should also be mentioned. Theirs is a job which goes largely unsung but without them the *QE2* would not be run so efficiently.

Amongst the others whom I would wish to thank are the authors of various invaluable books namely: Messrs. Potter and Frost ('QE2 - the Authorised Story') and Messrs. Flayhart and Warwick for their highly informative 'QE2'.

To the following, along with their organisations where applicable, I also say thank you for either their time and patience during my interrogation or for loaning precious photographs or artefacts: Fabian Acker (editor of 'Motor Ship'), Wally Adams, Brian Atkinson, Mr. Ballard (Sales Director GEC Electrical Projects Ltd), Bob Bantock, Len Betts, John T. Brown, Wyn Coombe, Robert Cove, Audrey and Steve Dymock, Barney Gallagher, George Gardner, Lilian Gibson, Bob Bruce Grice, Les Gough, Thomas Gough, John Havers, Imperial War Museum, Norman Jackman, Jim Jone, Diana Johnston (of MacGregor-Navire Publications Ltd.), P.A. Kroehenst, Sylvia Lee, Katherine Leiper (daughter of John Rannie), Terry Little (ex-Cunarder and incorrigable enthusiast who welcomes all fellow ex-Cunarders at the 'Eldon Arms', Southsea), Commodore Geoffrey Marr, Gordon Matthews (GEC Turbines Ltd.), Bill Miller of New Jersey, Nigel Overton and his staff at Southampton Maritime Museum (especially Simone), Southampton Central Library, Liz Stevens, Alma Topen (University of Glasgow), Peter Vasey (Scottish Records Office), Cedric Wasser, John Watson (MAN-B & W Diesels Ltd.), and Captain Robin Woodall.

My publisher, Roger Hardingham, I commend for his patience and my wife, Sandy, I thank for her encouragement, reminders of deadlines and for 'holding the fort'.

Bibliography

Arnott, Captain Robert, 'Captain of the Queen' (New English Library, 1982)
Bonsor, N.R.P., 'North Atlantic Seaway, Vol. 1' (David & Charles, 1975)
Cunard - 'The Cunarders 1840-1969' (Peter Barker Publishing Ltd.) Pleasure Island (1969?) - 'Sailing into a Great Tradition', 1982 World Cruise Souvenir Book
Hutchings, David F., 'RMS Queen Mary - 75 Years of Splendour' (Kingfisher Railway Productions, Southampton, 1986)
Hyde, Frances E., 'Cunard and the North Atlantic' (The Macmillan Press Ltd., 1975)
Johnson, Howard, 'The Cunard Story' (Whittet Books, 1987)
Kludas, Arnold, 'Passenger Ships of the World, Vol. 5 1951-1976' (Patrick Stephens, Cambridge 1977)
Lloyd Werft, Bremerhaven, 'Queen Elizabeth 2 - The History of a Conversion'
Marr, Commodore Geoffrey, 'The Queens and I' (Adlard Coles)
Maxtone Graham, John, 'Tribute to a Queen' (Berlitz Publications, 1987)
Miller, William H. 'Great Cruise Ships and Ocean Liners from 1954 to 1986' (Dover, 1988)
Miller, William H. 'Transatlantic Liners 1945-1980' (David & Charles, 1981)
Miller, William H. and Hutchings, David F., 'Transatlantic Liners at War - The Story of the Queens' (David & Charles, 1985)
Potter, Neil and Frost, Jack 'Queen Elizabeth 2 - The Authorised Story' (Harrap, 1969)
Ransome-Wallis, P., 'North Atlantic Panorama 1900-1976' (Ian Allan, 1977)
Rentell, Philip, 'Historic Cunard Liners' (Atlantic, 1986)
Smallpeice, Sir Basil, 'Of Comets and Queens' (Airlife, 1980)
Southampton Corporation, 'The Queens' (Harvey Barton - St. Stephens Publication, 1969)
Taylor, Arthur, 'Great Liners' (Southern Newspapers)
Villar, Captain Roger, 'Merchant Ships at War' (Conway/Lloyds of London Press, 1984)
Wall, Robert, 'Ocean Liners' (Collins, 1978)
Warwick, Ronald and Flayhart, William, 'QE2' (Norton, 1985)
Williams David and de Kerbrech, Richard, 'Damned by Destiny' (Teredo Books Ltd., 1982)

Newspapers

Daily Telegraph. Portsmouth News. The Times. Southern Evening Echo.

Journals and Periodicals

Bremerhaven Magazine No. 79, Mai/April 1987. Cruise Digest Reports, Vol. 6 Special Issue No. 1 1987. CME (Journal of Chartered Mechanical Engineers) May 1987. Diesel and Gas Turbine Worldwide Engineering, 13 Dec 1968. 100 A1 (Journal of Lloyds Register of Shipping) July 1986, Lloyds Ship Manager, May 1987. ME/LOG, August 1986. MacGregor-Navire News, April 1986. Marine Propulsion, Special Issue 'Rebirth of a Queen' May 1987. MPS Review, Sept. 1986. Motor Ship, The, June 1987. Naval Architect, The (Journal of the Royal Institution of Naval Architects), June 1986, June 1987. Sea Breezes. Ships Monthly. Shipbuilding and Shipping Record (especially Supplement 31 Jan. 1969). Shipping World and Shipbuilder.